The Unmaking of a
Hollywood Therapist

Annie Coe Toor

Ms. Coe Toor achieves in her memoir the Emersonian philosophy of *Self-Reliance*: if one tells a personal truth it resonates as a universal truth. Through her immersive prose, we journey gracefully through worlds that couldn't be more diametrically opposed and yet somehow important parallels are drawn between the maddening and absurd business of movie-making and the life-saving work of psychotherapy. The chapters on Orson Welles and Adrian Lyne are a highlight in this deeply moving memoir of a true English rose.

— *Yvonne Zima, screenwriter*

I love it! It works — British girl moves to Hollywood, has many fun, lighthearted adventures, and some sad ones, many great people are known and experienced, and all is told with a sharp sense of humor, the mood shifting with the Southern California weather — sunny, beautiful, a landscape to walk into, a pool to dive into. A significant career is built over many hardships — and then, finally she is bought down, a career ended, by a *single incident*. And truth be told, it is not fair; she could have avoided it all if not for her personal sense of rigorous honesty when she checked one fateful little box on a professional license renewal application. . . but so it goes. It is the ultimate injustice, but we know it is not a just world. Yet there's a lesson here: Even in an unjust world, one can keep one's soul."

— *Robert George, photographer*

The Unmaking of a
Hollywood
Therapist

Annie Coe Toor

*"Constant success shows us but one side of the world;
adversity brings out the reverse of the picture."*
— Charles Caleb Cotton

Timberlake Press
WOODLAND HILLS, CALIFORNIA

Cover Photo: Bruce Chevillat
Cover Design: Jade Design
Editor: Sylvia Cary, Cary Editorial & Book Consulting
Proofreader: Ann Hedrick, PhD
Author photo: ProPhoto, Glendale, California

ISBN-13: 978-0-692-75241-8
ISBN 10: 0-692-75241-2

Published in the United States of America
Timberlake Press
PO Box 129
Woodland Hills, California, 91365, USA

DEDICATION

Dedicated to my dearest, late husband, Bruce Toor, for his constant loving support and encouragement, as well as to my wonderful and nourishing circle of family and friends.

This book is also dedicated to my skilled, creative and patient editor, Sylvia Cary, who always made me feel that this book was worth doing, and without whom it would still be just a printout in a three-ring binder on a shelf.

Also, thank you, Bruce Chevillat, my longtime friend, for taking the photograph on that day in 1992 when I received my license to practice psychotherapy. A momentous occasion.

Additional thanks to Kim Sauvie, for her editorial help on earlier drafts of this book, and for more than once coming to my rescue when I called her with frustrating computer problems.

My deepest appreciation to my therapist, Angela, who guided and supported me over two decades. Her skills inspired me to move towards high education and ultimately to my new dream career as a licensed psychotherapist.

My thanks to Michael Goch, one of my attorneys throughout my ordeal. His kindness and concern were invaluable, as was his understanding acceptance of the decision I ultimately made to resolve my legal and professional dilemma.

And a special thanks to my "advance copy" readers, Yvonne Zima and Robert George, for their most valuable feedback.

And finally, my gratitude to Leo, Buffy, Slinky, and China, my family of four black cats, for keeping me company and comforted as I wrote this book.

CONTENTS

PART I
(2008)
The Unmaking of a
HOLLYWOOD
THERAPIST

PART II
(1965-2008)
The Making of a
HOLLYWOOD
THERAPIST

PART III
(2009-2011)
BACK TO...
The Unmaking of a
HOLLYWOOD
THERAPIST

Part I
(2008)

The Unmaking of a
Hollywood
Therapist

With weekly therapy and an antidepressant prescribed by a psychiatrist colleague, my client eased out of her isolation and gradually re-connected with many people she had known previously — producers, casting agents, fellow actors. She began walking with a new energy, her face glowing, framed by hair, now silver, and scraped up into a chic bun. Today she was dressed in a stylish, fuchsia-colored suit.

"You look so different," I said.

"Guess what? I'll be working again in two weeks. I got a supporting role in a feature and it's quite a big part."

"I'm happy for you."

"I can never thank you enough, Annie! You've guided me through this wretched darkness."

"You did the work," I told her. And she had. I wasn't just saying that to be modest. It was always a pleasure for me as a therapist when a client had the courage to do what it takes to reach a desired goal. It was one of the things that made me love my work.

After she left, I relaxed with another mug of tea and a handful of natural, unsalted almonds. I wrote down a few questions to suggest to the NBC reporter who was due any moment to interview me for a segment of a TV show called *Celebrity Live.*

Then came the expected tap on the door.

I opened it and greeted Mark and his cameraman. "Good to see you both again."

While they were setting up, I dashed into the bathroom to gussy up and powder my face so I wouldn't look glossy under the lights. I returned just in time for Mark to check his sound and attach a small microphone to my shirt. I sat down in one of the Victorian chairs.

"Perfect," Mark said. "Know you're busy. We'll try for just one take. Okay, let's do it." He faced the camera: "I am

Mark Wilson. This is *Celebrity Live.* Today we are in Burbank, in the heart of the media district, and once again we are in the elegant office of psychotherapist-to-the-stars, Annie Coe, whose specialty, as you might have guessed, is treating celebrities. That sounds like a pretty cool specialty, Annie." In a joking way, he lowered his voice and asked, "So tell me, who are some of the big-name celebrities you see in therapy?"

I laughed. "Come on, Mark! You know I can't tell you that! *Confidentiality.* I could lose my therapist's license for doing that."

"We wouldn't want to have that happen. Moving right along, you were telling us last week that you originally got into this field after writing your graduate school master's thesis on celebrity stress."

"I did. Before grad school I'd spent years working in the movie industry, and I saw the 'stress' part first-hand, and I experienced it, as they say, up close and personal. Nobody else was writing about it, so I decided to base my thesis on a study I did which included in-depth interviews with ten filmmakers and their spouses, and they gave me so much information. The thesis got quite a bit of attention in the industry. Many found it very helpful. And that's what eventually led me into this field."

"I should think *all* therapists would want to treat celebrities — see what they're really like."

I laughed again. "It's like we were saying during our last interview, celebrities are people, too. While it's sometimes startling to see a famous face walk into your office, the moment they start opening up, they're just like any other patient, trying to cope with daily life and a particular set of circumstances. In my practice, I get to see them all — from the A-list celebrities to people who are still desperate to make it and are depressed because they haven't.

"They may actually be very talented, but talent isn't enough. It's more to do with temperament, with attitude. Sadly, I see people that I just know won't make it in what's often a chaotic, judgmental Hollywood scene. Each one is unique. Some love the attention and adulation and being on the set, like the actor who once described a movie set as 'being in a playpen for adults.' Others hate it, hide out wherever they are, and can't wait to get enough money in the bank so they can quit and regain their privacy and anonymity."

"How do these folks know to call *you* to the rescue?"

"Most are referred to me by friends and colleagues who know that I worked in the industry. That helps a lot. I've been in their shoes. I know that show business is both exciting and stressful. It's unpredictable, competitive, and there are often long periods of unemployment, so it's either feast or famine with long, erratic hours and location shoots. Or the production may close down because they ran out of money. All that is stressful and hard on your family and your social life. When clients know that I *know* these things from personal experience, it makes them feel understood."

"Is that why you're a therapist now? Steady work?"

"That's a big part of it, Mark!"

"So what do you tell these people?"

"What I'd tell anybody in any stressful situation: find ways to get perspective. 'It's only a movie,' some like to say, or 'This too shall pass.' Then there's self-care."

"What's that?"

"Just as it sounds. Take care of your*self* — the temple of the soul as some call it. Healthy diet. Learn how to breathe correctly. Get enough sleep. Exercise. Emotional support from others — such as talking to a therapist. All these things are the basics that make things go so much better. Even for celebrities. Being a celebrity doesn't make you immune from being a human being."

Mark clapped his hands. "Bravo! You have such a nice, clear way of saying things. That's why we like to come and talk with you. No wonder you've got such a busy practice. So thank you, Annie Coe. Your insights into the human heart are so valuable. Unfortunately, we're out of time for today. See you next time."

They packed up quickly, thanked me again, and cleared out of my office.

No sooner had they left than the phone on my desk rang. Instead of letting the answering service get it, I picked up.

"Annie Coe's office, Annie Coe speaking."

"Annie Coe, the psychotherapist?"

"This is she. May I ask who is calling?"

"Dani. My name is Dani. I would like to make an appointment to see you. Soon. Very soon, if you have any time available." The halting, trembling voice I heard radiated anxiety, perhaps depression. I could hear how close she was to hanging up the phone in a fit of agitation.

"I can see you at three this afternoon. I had a cancellation. Or later on in the week, Thursday or Friday, at noon." I usually left those hours open for an emergency — or lunch.

"Today at three."

"Splendid. Do you need the address?"

"I have it. I was referred to you by..." and she named a popular celebrity. "I can talk to you about things, right? You can't sell what I say to the tabloids?"

"What we discuss is entirely confidential," I assured her. "May I ask why the urgency to see me?"

"I'm afraid to go out. I need help with this fear. I don't want to talk about it on the phone. Is it okay if I explain the rest at my appointment?"

"Of course. I'll see you at three, Dani."

Dani, as she had called herself, was a newly famous celebrity, only 24. I recognized her the minute she walked in, but we agreed she'd be "Dani." She was a star whose glamorous looks were displayed across billboards and splashed on magazine covers. In person she looked frail and drawn. What had happened to her?

"I had no idea that I would achieve my dream," she said, sitting down primly in one of the straight-back Victorian chairs, "and now this disturbing change in my life. It feels threatening to have people always watching me, ready to pounce and bully me. I feel like a trapped animal, hunted continuously."

"Sounds frightening," I said, compassionately.

"Do you mind, um, checking the windows for spies before we start talking?" she asked.

"Spies?"

"And the door, to be sure no one is listening or recording? I call them spies, the paparazzi."

I assumed her anxiety was building into paranoia, but when I looked out the window and saw a man with a camera across the street, watching my front office doors, I understood the reason for her feeling of being "hunted continuously."

"There might be a tabloid journalist outside."

I paused to watch Dani hold her stomach and start to rock back and forth, biting her lips.

"I need to go. But they're going to see me leave — from a psychologist's office," she groaned, sheer fear taking over.

"Take long, deep breaths, Dani, to help you calm down. Clear your mind. Feel your pulse even out, and your heart start to beat slower..."

Her color returned, and she even managed a genuine smile. "Wow. That worked really fast."

"I'm glad to hear it."

"I didn't mean to offend you before, with what I said about being in a psychologist's office. I just meant, it would be bad to see headlines that read — "

"I understand," I said.

She started to hyperventilate again.

"To help ease your mind about confidentiality..." I explained to her, in detail, how I was bound by the many laws of psychotherapy. Our relationship was absolutely confidential, though I did have to note the dates and times of her appointments with me. I was also required, by law, to report intent by my clients to commit suicide or homicide. "My files are always locked in a cabinet."

"But what if a journalist arrived at your office to question you about me?"

"I would not be allowed to say that you are my client, or that you are not my client."

She visibly relaxed. "I feel I can trust you. I have to. I have to get my life back together. You're going to help me be less afraid, right? I won't have to live like this for long, anyway, right? I can appear on camera again soon as—*me*?"

Dani was not the first patient to expect me to wave the psychotherapist's magic wand, which would cure them entirely, in our first session.

"I can teach you some techniques to cope with the added stress and pressure, and the anxiety you feel, and together we can determine how much of your fear is real and what may be over the top and perhaps triggered by something else in your life you aren't aware of now, but will uncover here in our sessions."

I listened to Dani's many stories of herself, often irrelevant to the reasons she had sought professional help, but I hoped that a foundation of trust and honesty would emerge so that her suffering could be explored and alleviated. In her quest to remain a famous celebrity, she had started to drink and smoke more. She had purchased a luxury car, a home in Beverly Hills, had overspent on lavish clothes, hair, makeup, tanning, anything to feel proactive in her celebrity role, and to feel more worthy. When I pressed her about her drinking, she admitted to drinking two full bottles of wine, daily, so I encouraged her to attend AA and gave her the names of some of the smaller out-of-the way meetings favored by celebrities who knew they'd be less likely to be hounded by photographers in such places.

Dani seemed convinced that stars inevitably end up disappointing their fans, somehow shocking and alienating their audience. In her head, she had herself a "has-been" by age twenty-five, or having a breakdown from the pressures of fame.

I understood. I described to her an experience I'd once had working as Robert Mitchum's assistant on a TV film, *One Shoe Means Murder.* He had learned over decades to take his fame in stride. When the film wrapped, I had escorted Robert to the Los Angeles Airport, and as we approached the barriers to the public areas, mobs of fans and media awaited us.

"Well, Annie, ready?" he said in that distinctive baritone voice.

"I suppose," I said, shaking in fear.

A mass of reporters pushed and shoved to get closer. Cameras were aimed at our faces, lightbulbs flashed and blinded our eyes. Fans yelled for autographs and tried to grope him. Like a swarm of buzzing locusts, they yelled for him, "Robert... Bob... Mitch... Mr. Mitchum... here, look here!"

A security guard helped us break away from the crowd, but we were chased to the limousine. With the chauffeur's aid, we scrambled inside onto the plush seats. I was terrified to be in the midst of such a threatening throng. Only the dark tint of the windows subdued the flashes of white lights. Robert's cool, accepting demeanor, achieved over years of experience, enabled him to handle the hysteria with ease, even humor. I gasped for breath to survive my anxiety. We sped away from the crowd into the safety of darkness. I had only been his assistant, I told her, so I could not begin to imagine coping with a life of fame. I promised we would partner up and help her get through this with grace, not panic. "It's doable, Dani, and you can do it."

At the end of our first session together, Dani scheduled three more, ending up seeing me for nine months before deciding to "take a break." I told her she was welcome to come back for a "tune-up" whenever she wanted, which is what I offer everybody. As human beings, we are never "finished." Learning the art of living is something we keep on doing until our last breath.

Yes, I loved my work. It had taken me years to figure out what I wanted to be when I grew up. I wasn't one of those people who knew they wanted to be dentists by the time they were three. For me, it was an onion-peeling process — layer by layer — each time closer and closer to my core. But little did I know on this particular day that even though I had finally found my core, that wasn't going to be the end of it.

Chapter 2

A DRINK WITH AN OLD FRIEND

I phoned Bruce, my husband, from my office to remind him I'd be home a little later than usual because I was meeting Tony for a drink. Tony was a colleague and we'd been two of 17,000 volunteers after Hurricane Katrina where we'd counseled those who were experiencing post-traumatic stress from the event. As Red Cross volunteers, known as Disaster Mental Health Counselors, we were deployed to the Astrodome in Houston where thousands of evacuees were sheltered after the catastrophe in New Orleans. I had been drawn to Tony because of his genial nature, his sensitivity, and depth of compassion. He and I had become instant friends, supporting and caring for one another in the midst of the heartbreak around us.

We had arrived to offer aid to the nineteen thousand evacuees, whose numbers swelled more and more each day. Busloads of volunteers had arrived — doctors, nurses, aides, food and cleanup workers, registration and information volunteers, religious fanatics, and others I couldn't classify. There had been thousands of police, officials, and National Guard in their camouflage uniforms, many with M-16's.

Once I received my I.D cards and clearance, I fought my way through police barricades, security checks, television trucks and cameras, and photographers, to reach the staircase alongside the huge ramp going down to the Astrodome floor.

We were met with a deafening cacophony of delivery trucks — food, clothing, and ice — waste management vans, ambulances, electric carts, military and paramedic vehicles, all roaring up and down the ramp.

Tony and I spent a lot of time with the volunteers and paid workers, evaluating if they were burned out or overwhelmed, and if they needed a day off, or to return home. We met many unique people from across the nation and Canada, many whom had given up their jobs or taken vacation time, or spent their own money, leaving the security of their families and homes to devote themselves to this cause.

Once the buses from New Orleans began arriving, there were 28 thousand evacuees housed in the Astrodome. The Astrodome floor was chock-a-block with thousands of green cots squeezed together in any available space. Most came from the "hell" of the Super Dome where rapes, murder, and beatings were seen and reported. Despite all of their losses, most of the survivors were grateful to be alive, and to have food and shelter. After a few days, many more facilities were in operation. Computers were brought in, the first sign of technology in an area that had regressed to a primordial way of life.

I must have walked miles each day passing out water and food snacks, and listening to the evacuees' stories of grief and loss, some evacuees too shocked or frightened to speak, which helped open communication between us. I gave out extra blankets and cleaned up malodorous messes. I did crisis counseling and problem solving. I helped register hundreds waiting to get into the shelter, many wailing and grief-stricken. They had no homes, no cars, no jobs, no money or identification, no clothing or belongings. I worked with other volunteers, including Tony, to reunite families, friends, and even pets.

The loudspeaker system had constantly blared important announcements. When a missing person had been located, hundreds clapped, cheered, and cried. It felt like a moment of magic. The humanity of it all was profound, palpable, rippling through the Astrodome, the evacuees expressing gratitude, love, and courage. Nothing has compared, then or since.

Eighty-five showers and hundreds of toilets were installed. Now relieved to be at the Astrodome after their horrific experience at the Superdome in New Orleans, the evacuees were mainly well-behaved, perhaps due to the heavy police and army presence. I saw several scuffles and fights between evacuees, usually because one person left their cot and returned to find a stranger had taken that place. The cots and their location became precious territory, especially when a group of evacuees became friends, forming new "families." I did not see or hear of violent crimes during my deployment there and was impressed by the accepting behavior and camaraderie exhibited by all. Phone banks, FEMA offices, post offices, information areas, Veteran's Administration and Social Security offices, transportation, missing person's databases, and other resources were hastily built, designed to help bring some stability to those who had none. Other facilities were slow to be organized, but the evacuees were remarkably patient.

I was impressed by the overall organization — the food area supplied meals several times a day until 8 pm. Huge quantities of clothing and shoes were available, and any person who was missing medication could have it replaced free of charge. Medical care was constantly available, even for those who needed to continue methadone therapy.

Some evacuees, despite their anguish, helped the volunteers to keep areas clean. They were accepting of their fate, patiently waiting and hoping for loved ones to surface. Magical moments occurred when the loudspeaker announced the name of a missing person who had just been located — the crowd responding with screeches of joy and cheers.

The stadium lighting dimmed at night but never faded to complete dark. To me, this was the twilight zone. Phone banks were installed for people to make free long-distance phone calls. Continental airlines set up several computers and whenever possible, arranged free flights to any state where a relative was waiting.

Outside the Astrodome, the Houston police and Harrison County sheriffs controlled traffic, a steady stream of cars filled with would-be volunteers and those searching for family and friends. The entrances were heavily guarded from religious fanatics, bibles in hand, clamoring to get inside and offer God and peace to all those suffering. And we were warned that drug dealers were waiting to pounce, but they were stopped by the police. The security inside and outside was tight, and no one could enter unless they had a pink wristband (meaning they were an evacuee) or had proof of being a relative, or they were a credited television crew member, journalist, or celebrity (to help or to donate). Otherwise, no one was allowed thorough the barricades.

It was a massive operation — chaotic at first, but it gradually became more organized as each hour passed. It was a catastrophe that showed me the power of people pulling together with courage and acceptance.

At 2:00 a.m. one night I was on watch and walking the floor when a potentially ugly scene began to unfold. I saw the battalion fire chief and a big group of his firemen about to ascend the walkways which went to the top of the Astrodome. I could tell they were on a mission. I stopped the chief and asked what was happening.

"There are too many people who have set up in the walkways, which is against the fire department rules and poses a major threat to their own safety and to the Astrodome," he said. "I need to move all those people out and back down to the floor."

With all the authority I could muster, I confronted him. "It's 2:00 a.m. in the morning. There are babies and children in those families. Stop your mission. If you have to continue during daylight hours, then get clearances from all the department heads and the medical staff. These families have suffered enough."

After a lot of persuasion, the chief and his crew acquiesced for the night. I was relieved to have been there for what could have been anther scene of horror for so many families.

All these scenes from the past played in my head as I waited for Tony at a mahogany table by a window in a bar overlooking Ventura Boulevard. It was late afternoon, but still sunny and warm in the San Fernando Valley. I was giddy at the thought of seeing Tony again. Our friendship had been reduced to telephone conversations, six years of them without a proper meeting. I couldn't believe it had already been that long since Katrina.

Tony rushed over to me, all smiles and hugs. "Annie! You haven't changed at all!"

"You have more grey hair!"

"You're as slim as ever, and what an outfit! Sleek, chic, quite a difference from the Red Cross apron. How did your TV interview go?"

"Very well." We took our seats. "Those years of hard work to get my psychotherapy license seem to have finally paid off!"

"I caught you on one of those interviews you do about Hollywood and how hard it is to be rich and famous. Must be rough! But I was so excited. 'I know her!'"

Growing uncomfortable with so much attention, I changed the subject 180 degrees. "Has your wife's broken ankle healed?"

"She's fully mobile again, running after the kids."

I had never felt the desire to have children of my own, yet I was happy that Tony seemed so content. The barman brought an ice bucket for our bottle of Chardonnay, and a cut glass filled with peanuts and almonds. Tony and I clinked glasses with gusto, toasting our friendship. He hadn't changed, still as warm and straightforward as always.

"Do you ever miss it?" he asked.

"Katrina?"

He nodded. "I think of it a lot. I'll remember those two weeks for the rest of my life."

"It was the highlight of my career as a therapist."

"But you're happy in your practice now?" he asked.

"Very! You should see my fancy office."

Tony laughed, accepting me as charming rather than boastful. He checked his watch, then we agreed to order another bottle of wine.

"But I don't think I will ever be so moved as when we climbed down the last few stairs to the floor of the Astrodome, stricken when we saw the thousands of evacuees on cots. Nothing could ever compare to that."

"Do you remember the two teenage girls who spent hours on a rooftop clinging to each other against the wind? They were traumatized, and who could blame them? They saw friends and relatives floating in the water below them," he recalled.

"They were lucky — saved by one of the rescue helicopters, along with thousands of others."

"I remember the elderly man in a wheelchair who saw his wife of fifty years fall into the water and drown," I said, tearing up even more. "He never complained, simply asked for Listerine because he hadn't brushed his teeth in two days."

"Endless stories of courage," he added.

"I don't know about you, but for me it was a difficult adjustment going home and back to work with clients in show business. A big leap from Katrina," I said.

"Yes, it was. I was depressed for a good many months."

"I felt depressed and irritable. Vulnerable. No one in L.A. seemed ruffled by Katrina, or anything for that matter, other than their daily, inconsequential challenges, or at least that's how I saw it," I said.

"Same thing for me. I was annoyed with routine work and trivial talk," Tony went on.

"Debriefing by the Red Cross in Houston and in L.A helped me adjust to my old, well, old-newly altered life," I tried to explain.

"Yes, I went through debriefing, as well. The memories, you know?" he asked.

"I know," I said.

As we continued to reminisce over the many intimate personal tragedies, it felt as though I was grieving for them all over again. We talked for several hours until Tony looked at his watch again and sat up straight, reaching in his pocket for his wallet.

"I gotta get going if I'm going to make my flight back to Salt Lake." He put bills on the table, corked the half bottle of wine that was left over, and we rushed out to the parking lot.

After Tony put the bottle of wine in my trunk, we hugged good-bye.

"Drive safe," he said as he jumped into his rental car. "Let's not wait another six years before we do this again."

   I waved as he pulled out of the parking lot and headed off towards the Los Angeles Airport.

Chapter 3

ARREST

Minutes after I got onto the freeway for the short drive to my Hollywood Hills home, still thinking about my conversation with Tony, a police car with a shrill siren suddenly appeared behind me.

Maybe it's not directed at me, I told myself. If I kept driving, he would leave me alone. He was simply trying to get past me. I changed lanes to be out of his way, envisioning an escaped prisoner on the road and the potential car chase I was about to see unfold before me.

Blinding red lights flashed in my rearview mirror. I couldn't believe a highway patrol car was on my tail.

"Exit at the next ramp, Woodman," commanded an ominous voice through a megaphone or bullhorn. The flashing lights followed me down the ramp.

I trembled all over, my heart racing in my chest. Icy terror inched up into my throat. I wanted to floor the gas pedal and fly down the fast lane. It was only minutes before I would be home. But the sound of sirens shrieked around me, drowning out my desperately concocted escape plan. I was driving in the slow lane, well within the speed limit.

"Stop your car at the red curb."

The patrol car slowed to a stop behind my black Jaguar. The voice ordered me to stay in my vehicle. *What had I done?* When I put my car into park, I felt faint. If I did faint, would that prompt the officer to feel sorry for me? Would he let me go on the grounds that I was near hysterics and to harass me would be cruel? I tried to take deep breaths as his flashlight shined through the back of my window, and moved toward my driver's side window. Surely he had seen my panicked expression. The truth would be revealed soon. I comforted myself with the thought of being home, feeding my cats, and getting some much-needed sleep.

A California Highway Patrol officer appeared at my window. "License and registration," he ordered.

I fumbled with my wallet to remove the license from its slot. My gaze was immediately drawn to the weapon at his hip. "Our bobbies don't carry guns," I said, handing him my information.

"Where are you from?" the officer paused for a moment, giving me hope.

"England," I replied.

"You're in America now, ma'am," he said. I watched as he strode back to his car to run my license through their criminal database.

Ha, ha, I grinned to myself, I had a clean record. Not a blemish on me in the system. After what seemed an hour, the officer returned.

"You were weaving over the freeway lanes. Exit the car, ma'am."

Exit the car? He wanted me to get out? Unheard of! Did he want to pat me down? He had a gun, and a Billy club! I started to wonder if he really was a law enforcement officer. I had heard stories of psychotic cop-lookalikes. But he had run my plate and license number. He knew I was Annie Coe, a psychotherapist to celebrities, a lecturer, volunteer disaster mental health counselor, and a recognized humanitarian. What could I possibly have done?

"My eyes only left the road for a moment or two to adjust..."

He looked impatient as he repeated, "Exit the car."

I released my seat-belt and clambered out of my vehicle, realizing that I was dizzy and unsteady. I was confused, convinced I hadn't had any impairment as I said goodbye to Tony in the parking lot outside the bar. What was happening? Was one of my tail lights out? I was afraid to check, wary of the impatient policemen and his weapons.

Could it be that I drank too much? The question was a whisper in my mind, immediately dismissed. Tony and I had shared a bottle and a half of wine over two hours. I was used to drinking wine. I couldn't be tipsy. To be pulled over by the police would make anybody wobbly, I reassured myself. I had never been in such a humiliating position before, being ordered about and spoken to as though I were a criminal. I had eased many clients through moments of panic and paranoia, yet all my years of studying had apparently been for nothing.

It was no time for an emotional breakdown.

I was startled by the second officer who emerged from nowhere. He ordered me to remove my shoes. Too dumbfounded to ask why, I leaned on a nearby newspaper stand to remove my new, black patent leather heels, which cramped my toes. I had dressed up for my reunion in a Chinese printed, raw silk shirt, black tailored trousers, and drop gold earrings. It was a rare occasion for me to take time off and reschedule clients. I didn't usually dress like this.

The officers suspected I was driving under the influence of alcohol. Questions they asked about the day and date, I answered accurately. Then the lead officer handed me a 3 x 5 inch index card and a pen. He instructed me to print out my name and the alphabet. Using the newsstand as a surface, I tried to comply, but the index card seemed to slip all over the blue metal lid. I damned the paint, the wind, the officers for having me perform such an insipid task. I chased the small rectangle of paper, trying to steady myself and hold the pen, to write what they had asked. I could feel them peering over my shoulder. My face felt hot, vulnerability swamping me with every new truck and car that zoomed by. The light blue lines blurred in and out of focus as I struggled to keep the letters neatly in a row. I had gone to graduate school for two years. My degrees were framed, from my Associate's degree all the way to my M.A, yet I was unable to formulate the alphabet in my mind, let alone remember how to write the letters.

I'd had three, maybe four glasses of wine, but no food in my tummy all day except for the nuts in the bar. The realization left me terrified. *Keep your eyes and ears open at all times.* That was one of my Dad's many rules, which I tried to always practice. But I hadn't done this when I left the bar. I admitted to myself that I had lacked complete awareness of my state as I had gotten behind the wheel.

"Blow into this," commanded the officer, handing me a plastic pipe with an attached mouthpiece. I stared at the breathalyzer, wanting to yell, "No!" but instinct warned me not to cause trouble. He could cart me off to jail and keep me locked up indefinitely.

Jail. I could not believe it. Nightmarish. I blew with as much fresh air as I could muster. He took the pipe from my shaking hand and peered at the measurement gauge on the tube.

"Your blood alcohol level is over the legal limit," he declared.

In a feeble attempt at humor, I grinned and said, "That gizmo can't be accurate!"

The officer shook his head with a serious expression, as if to say, "Lady, this is no joke."

I had been used to getting what I wanted by exaggerating my British accent, by using humor or by being flirtatious. Nothing helped me now. I latched onto their appearances, both patrol men sporting mustaches, one tall and slim with a finely chiseled face, aquiline nose. Perhaps he was on TV. Had I seen him in anything? Could I know him? Most actors in L.A. had second jobs.

Don't ask him, Annie. Shut up and be careful. You are not yourself.

His partner, double-chinned and burly, made me wonder what had happened to the strict, sleek, weight limit for officers. More lax rules and regulations these days, at least in some things. My mind wandered around until it was jarred back into reality by the officer's serious announcement.

"On November 19, 2008, at 18:24 hours, you are formally charged with driving under the influence of alcohol."

I was arrested, not just for being under the influence, but also for weaving across the freeway and making unsafe lane changes. I trembled as the officer rattled off my rights.

Handcuffed and carefully guided by a hand pushing down on my head, I lurched into the back seat of the patrol car which pulled away from the curb and on towards the Van Nuys jail — just like one sees on telly or in the movies. I tried to realize that the scene was real. Questions and worries tumbled about in my head. What would happen to my car, abandoned in the red zone? I wanted to shed the ugly feeling in my soul. *Let me go home to safety!* In several minutes, a large, neon blue "Police Station" sign loomed before my eyes. One of the officers helped me wriggle out of the back seat, difficult to accomplish with my hands cuffed behind my back. Flanked by an officer on each side, I was led up several stairs into the entrance.

I wanted to die.

Chapter 4

STIFF UPPER LIP

Inside the police station, I was blinded by the harsh headache-inducing, bluish-green fluorescent ceiling lights which glared over a crowd of prisoners surrounded by policemen, sheriffs, and patrol officers. Their leather belts were laden with Billy clubs, military paraphernalia, and more guns and bullets than I had ever seen. Some officers wore khaki colors, while others were strapped into black uniforms. All of them had the same standard, high leather boots.

The building was not large. Certificates of different kinds were framed on the walls, signed by the mayor, by judges, and other important officials. The floor was tan, speckled, with simple metal benches welded to the ground, next to floor-to-ceiling glass windows.

At the first window, I answered personal questions.

"How long will I be detained?" I asked.

They ignored me. I wanted to curl into a ball on the floor or ram my fists against the glass windows, until someone answered my questions. It may have been standard procedure for them, the "pass along" that they did so mechanically, but they rushed through everything so quickly, I had no time to adapt.

At the next window, my photo was taken. The infamous "mug shot," I presumed. Two flashes of very bright light resulted in two pictures, one of me facing them, the second in which they barked at me to, "Turn to the side."

The third window was even more traumatic. The officer who had been given my belongings earlier itemized all the contents of my purse — my cash, credit cards, and photos from my wallet, which he placed into a large, brown envelope. The list of items within was stapled to the outside.

"Take off your jewelry, please," he said.

"Do I have to?"

They were brusque. I removed my watch, earrings, and neck pendant. When he motioned for me to remove my gold and diamond wedding rings, I reluctantly twisted them off my fingers, seeing the pale line of skin left behind. The rings had become so much a part of me, I could not believe the police would confiscate them. "Let no man put asunder," was that not part of the wedding vows? I tried not to glare or cry as he listed my beloved items and slipped them into another brown envelope. I signed both lists.

"Will you please loosen my handcuffs now?" I asked.

One of the officers glanced over at me, yet neither of them replied. There was no use asking. I resigned myself to grin and bear it, the epitome of the British "stiff upper lip."

Next, I was directed to a table where another officer fingerprinted me. I watched as the black ink spread over my fingertips. The officer held my hand poised over the white paper and roughly rolled my finger pads over the page. He wiped the black ink away for me, ignoring me as I winced, the arthritis in my hands burning after his rough handling.

After being "processed," I was led further into the jail. Many of the prisoners were wearing gang garb: baggy pants, crotched at or below the knee, and oversized t-shirts in red or royal blue, the gang member colors which I remembered from working as an intern psychotherapist with kids on probation. Girls and women were dressed in skintight skirts and miniskirts, decorated with rhinestones and sequins. They wore tight-fitting tank tops with plunging necklines, their cleavage about to burst out, asses barely covered by arrays of patterned tights, garter belts, stockings and dangerously high stiletto heels. Layers of make-up, crowned by thick, pouty lips, covered in all colors of lipstick, even black. Angry, resigned expressions, jeering and cussing until finally reprimanded by officers.

I had to face the truth. I had committed a crime, like everyone else here. I had driven a car under the influence of alcohol. I realized what could have happened. Wreckage. Carnage. I could have gotten myself killed. Other innocent victims could have died because of me, simply because I hadn't checked myself before getting behind the wheel.

I was led past small, crowded jail cells to a larger one. To my relief, there was no one in it. The officer unlocked my handcuffs and the cell door before handing me a threadbare blanket.

Three dull grey walls; the fourth consisted of sickly green iron bars. A cot and a loo, barricaded off for privacy. The officer slammed the cell door shut and turned the key in the lock.

CLANG. The sound echoed down the corridor as he walked away.

Surely, I was trapped in a movie.

Chapter 5

ROLE REVERSAL

As I looked out through the bars of my jail cell, irony stuck me. There were many times I had been ushered through doors and gates at the San Bernardino County Juvenile Detention Center to interview teenagers, some of whom I cleared for residency at the Optimist Boys' Group Home in Devore. My purpose as lead therapist had been to work with teenagers who had never lived life without crime. It seemed an impossible task, getting them to confide in me, particularly those who had been loyal to gangs all their lives. An iota of trust was sometimes gained as I worked with their issues of drug and alcohol abuse, lack of impulse control, gang involvement, and repercussions from physical and sexual abuse. I learned to get really tough with those kids, to teach them and challenge them, but, most importantly, to let them know I cared.

What a role-reversal!

Alone for the first time since my arrest, I was frozen down to my bones in spite of the perspiration that beaded on my forehead. Dizziness overwhelmed me for long moments at a time, as I tried to understand what it meant to have a criminal record.

A buzzing sound roused me from my nearly catatonic state. Had someone been informed of my arrest? I waited, but none of the police officers came to free me. The air conditioning blasted down around me. I thrust the blanket around my shoulders, attempting to stop my shivers, and massaged my hands and wrists, the pain made worse by the frigid temperature. Riddled with shame and remorse, I counted seconds, minutes. How long would they hold me? Film images flashed through my mind. Darkness, slop for food, men in solitary confinement chalking off days and months on their cell walls. Armed guards. Exercise compounds. Electric fences with knotted barbed wire at the top. I shuddered in horror.

But what luck, about twenty-five feet away outside my cell, two large trashcans had been left, filled to the brim with grey blankets. The two policemen I asked to please get me another blanket refused to be bothered. Each request was gruffly denied. Eventually, a female police officer came by. I politely asked her for a blanket, in the hope that she would have more empathy than the men.

She faced me, with her nose through the bars. "Lady, where do you think you are? The Peninsula Hotel?"

I shook my head, appalled. My angry retorts were withheld, instinct reminding me to curb myself with blue-clad law enforcement.

"One prisoner, one blanket," she snarled before striding away.

An officer opened my cell door, but would not answer any of my questions. All of the police had adopted the same attitude, "Wait, you will find out." He led me to a telephone hanging on the wall. The area was open, and I felt horribly exposed with people staring out at me from their barred cells. Some were asleep or in a drugged daze, shivering on their metal-framed cots.

I pressed the appropriate buttons when prompted by the computer operator, finally dialing the number for my land-line home phone. My husband, Bruce, would be home — that is, if he picked up the phone instead of letting the answering machine take the message, as was his habit. He picked up the line!

"Are you all right, Annie? I've been worried about you. You've been gone for hours."

He liked to call me "the Jaguar of therapists." What would he think of me now?

"I'm in jail," I confessed, telling him the short version of my arrest. "I'm in Van Nuys."

"I'll be right there."

His voice was comforting. My husband, always protective and dependable. He would fix the problem, get me released, and out of the mess I had created.

Time passed. I paced around my cell in a futile effort to warm myself. It had been hours since my arrest; the clock read 10:30 pm. I wondered what had delayed Bruce. No one would give me any information. My mind constantly chattered on, revolving around my worries. I had clients scheduled to see me the next day. I wasn't sure where my car was, or the state of my driver's license. What would become of my career? I staved off another panic attack, feeling as though I had lost myself.

Chapter 6

YOU ARE FREE TO GO

Hours later I was awakened by the words, "You are free to go." A female cop was standing over my bed. "Pardon?"

"Pardon?" she sneered. "I said you are free to go."

She led me, half dazed, outside to the general waiting area. My dear husband sat on one of the metal benches, hands on his chin, using his cane as a leaning post. He hugged me as I sobbed against him.

We hardly spoke during the drive home, both of us depleted from the ordeal. Bruce turned on the heat. With my head leaning against his shoulder, we drove eight miles on the freeway, exited off the Barham Boulevard ramp, and wound our way up into the hills. I was greeted by the warmth of our home and our four furry black cats that circled and sniffed my legs, meowing for my attention.

I scarfed down a ham sandwich with a cup of hot tea as Bruce watched me, quietly.

"I'm so thankful you weren't hurt, Annie."

"Thank you for being there," I whispered, tears in my eyes.

"You're home now, where you belong," he said, warm with compassion.

I felt dirty, and a prolonged hot shower did nothing to wash away the ugly effects of my being imprisoned. I took three soft blankets from my linen closet, luxurious after my jail blanket of recycled materials. Slipping under the silk comforter of my bed, numbness swept over me. My ordeal was over, at least for the night.

Chapter 7

HOME

Haunting, distorted images of my arrest and the jail dominated my sleep. The hollow metallic sounds of cell doors slamming, keys ominously jangling on their rings as wardens locked prisoners away. No escape, and nothing to do but wait. Time stretched on and on, and endlessly on, as I slowly froze and broke down emotionally, mentally.

Impersonal officers watched, condemning me. I crouched in the darkest corner of my jail cell, trying very hard not to focus on the empty, pale patch of skin over my left ring finger. Terror.

I sat bolt upright, wide awake after the appalling nightmares. My heart thumped erratically, my pulse racing, cold with perspiration. Clutching the sheets, I attempted to ground myself, focusing purely on relaxation techniques. I was not who I thought I had been. I had become a criminal, soon to be sentenced by the court system. How could I have sunk to such a level? One mistake, and the decades of study and work were rendered meaningless. I felt a failure.

When Tony had called, I had had absolutely no hesitation about meeting him. Now I was playing the *'what if'* game — *what if* I had had drinks with Tony on another day; *what if* we had met earlier in the afternoon? *What if* I had remembered to eat an actual meal during the day, my busy schedule not an excuse for my lack of self-awareness? If any of those *what if* things had been the case, then this nightmare could have been avoided. I recognized the thoughts for what they were — a psychological reach, the processing of information through staunch denial. I could not deny how badly I'd erred, nor how fearful I was that "the worst" hadn't even happened yet.

A comforting dose of reality was Bruce, soundly asleep by my side, and my two long-haired black cats, scrunched in next to me. Leo's head rested against my thigh, Buffy in nirvana on her back, paws flopping about.

They helped soothe my mind, though I was devastated, knowing I had tarnished Bruce's image of me. I had become a disappointment in his eyes; though part of me knew my thoughts were part conjecture, I lacked the courage to ask him. He was always very proud of me, calling me the "Jaguar" of therapists, and sending admiring updates to our friends and relatives about my volunteer work with the evacuees from New Orleans right after Hurricane Katrina.

Our courtship had been easy, fun. It had begun with correspondence between us, starting after I responded to his ad in the *Classifieds* section of the newspaper. We penned one another a few times before we set a date, at *Pierre's,* a classy restaurant in Los Feliz Village. I had walked through the mahogany, beveled glass doors, and saw him sitting at the end of the bar. He stood to greet me, smiling broadly. My critical eye immediately leapt into operation. He wore neutral colors, plain perhaps, yet there was nothing about him that looked dowdy. He was tall, maybe 6'3," a striking yet humble presence.

Our conversation roamed back and forth easily, with both of us asking questions about each other's lives and histories. Despite my red flags about his three divorces, several health issues, and his being eleven years older than

I, an internal voice kept telling me to continue to get to know him.

"May I ask you a question?" I asked.

"Of course."

"You told me during one of our phone chats that you had been retired for a year from a law practice, and yet you were too busy to meet me for a month."

He laughed, a bit self-consciously. "Twenty-eight women replied to my ad and I drove all over L.A. for breakfasts, lunches and dinners. It was hectic. And exhausting!"

"You were really motivated! I hope it was worth all your time and energy."

"I met several interesting women, but many were truly eccentric or blatantly asked for legal advice. But you seem special."

Bruce was unpretentious, sensitive, and highly intelligent. I was excited that I liked him. After hugging in the parking lot, we planned a second date for the following weekend. My first Saturday night out in months.

Over many months, he courted me royally: scrumptious dinners at gourmet restaurants, elegant bouquets delivered to my office suite or home, lavish gifts. It was difficult learning to accept being spoiled, but finally I basked in it all. He had worked thirty-three years as a successful litigator in a downtown law practice, taking viola lessons as a release from courtroom stress and as an artistic non-confrontational outlet. A wise decision. Six years later he became a general partner at the firm and a sought-after classical musician. A healthy balance in his life.

I was excited to attend chamber music and symphony concerts with him, especially those in which he performed as a violist. I stepped into the auditorium, saw the musicians on stage, watching as the orchestra tuned up their instruments. I focused on Bruce as the conductor bowed to the jubilant audience. Silence. He raised his baton, and the concert began. I loved Bruce's expression of passion, music flowing out of his instrument, elegantly handsome in his tuxedo. The viola he held lightly balanced in the crook of his shoulder was a bright reddish-brown. His movements were fluid, and I marveled that such a strong man could call such delicate beauty from the slightly larger version of a violin. It was a new feeling to be proud in a relationship.

After only nine months, Bruce invited me on a ten-day cruise to Alaska, on the Crystal Symphony. The gracious staff showed us to our large suite. A queen-sized bed fitted with open drawers, enough space for our belongings. A small bathroom and shower. I liked the balcony, furnished with two lounge chairs and a table. I had brought two strings of mini-lights with me, using one strand to decorate the main room while the other I wove cheerfully around the rails of our balcony. Lodgings came with our very own butler who, at 5 p.m., delivered champagne with silver platters of shellfish and caviar and other exotic delicacies on ice. The food was always impeccably prepared and served, with crisp cloth napkins for our laps and perfectly polished silverware on the elegant table. Bruce and I took late-night walks on deck, stunned by Alaska at night, always happy to return to our suite with the twinkling mini-lights. During the day, we were surrounded by dramatic views of waterfalls, icebergs and wild animal life. I was in a dream, hoping never to wake up.

A secure and loving man. I was lucky. But then, so was he.

I wept inside.

Chapter 8

IMPOUND

Bruce studied the legal paperwork instead of reading the newspaper at breakfast, seated at our kitchen table. Sunlight streamed in through our picture windows. I could feel the warmth, yet the view failed to bring me my normal sense of contentment. Smells mingled together: Bruce's banana bread, his coffee billowing fragrant steam into the air. His toast was crisp, lightly buttered.

My stomach was in knots, rebelling when I thought of food. Whether Bruce noticed my agitation, or because he was not the type to procrastinate, he suggested we drive over to the impound yard to collect my car. Years of companionship between us had me wait to begin the longer, more detailed rehashing of my arrest. *Begin with the practical, before the emotional*, as my father used to say.

Bruce was quieter than usual, but I knew he would help me and wanted to.

En route to the impound lot, I read and re-read the directions, the paper crinkling in my nervous hands. The scenery changed from a polished neighborhood to a seemingly desolate area, with chain-link fences and shops with rusted window grates. The deserted buildings and barred-up liquor stores seemed depressing in the early morning hours. We made a turn off one of the main avenues to reach our destination and were met with further signs of squalor. Strip clubs dotted the street, their neon lights off for the day; auto body shops were guarded by monstrous guard dogs. Dumpsters everywhere were filled to their capacity, overflowing and circled by flies.

After reaching the lot, we joined nine other sullen-looking offenders, waiting in line to pay tow truck and impound fees. The mailbox outside the entrance had rust crawling up over its metal post and underbelly. Two men entered a bar across the street for their early morning fixes. A man in front of me grew louder, swearing more often, as he argued with the owner over fees. He was a burly man, his arms covered in tattoos.

"No payment, no car," the cashier repeated over and over again.

Thankfully, the man wanted his car more than he spoiled for a fight, so he paid. I approached the counter, wishing someone had been in front of me. Within moments, my sleek, black Jaguar was brought out to the holding area, which was as large as an airport hangar and jam-packed with cars of all makes and models. My car appeared to be unblemished, save for the storage license plate number they had painted in white on the front window shield.

"Shall I follow you?" I asked Bruce, both of us watching one of their workers scrape the white paint away.

"Of course," he replied. "I'll make sure we don't get separated."

"Thank you, your being close by will be reassuring."

I got into my Jag, my anxiety mounting as I saw those who were still waiting staring at me. My hands were shaking as I pulled on my seatbelt and drove nervously out of the impound lot, and headed for the freeway...

Part II
(1965-2008)

The Making of a
Hollywood
Therapist

Chapter 9

ETERNAL RAIN

Eternal rain. It dulled the senses. Gloomy, foreboding skies. Darkness crept into my bones. I imagined exotic islands where people stood in swimming pools for hours, reading books and sipping from tall, iced drinks, the rims laden with slices of Hawaiian fruits. Did people actually grumble about daily sunshine?

Our family lived in Southport, Lancashire, until I was about five years old. At summer's end, the cherry tree in the front garden exploded into pink blossoms. Nearby, pastoral green fields, dotted with cows and sheep, forests of silver birch trees, and joyous songs from mockingbirds all quieted my restlessness.

In our neighborhood, each garden shimmered with flowers from every color in a paint palette, all tended by loving hands. My perfectionist Dad was obsessed with ridding his two lawns of weeds; if he spied one amidst the emerald carpet, it provoked his Yorkshire ire. "If a job is worth doing, it is worth doing well," he stated repeatedly, trying to imprint his principle on our brains.

He ruled his family from the staunch position of power and authority in a traditional European patriarchal manner. I respected his strength, but was scared of him and yearned for warmth and affection. His enforced discipline was harsh and relentless, especially on my rebellious sister, Jacquie, which Dad later regretted. When he'd had enough, she was sent to her bedroom.

"Stay there until you have sorted yourself out!" Dad ordered sternly. She would slam the door, her screams dwindling to whimpers, staying in her room for hours. I hid under the stairs, shivering in fear, covering my ears, pretending nothing had happened until my frozen hands and feet sent me to find warmth.

Infrequently I managed to please my father, but usually my behavior and performance fell short of his high standards. I was not a quick learner, and if I did not immediately understand his explanations, Dad raised his eyebrows, his voice impatient and irritable, shaking his head in disgust at my ignorance. I ended up in tears, begging him to not judge me, and pleaded for him to leave me alone so I could do my homework on my own.

Crushing dissatisfaction coming from him and echoing from within myself led me to feel hopeless and resulted in a poor self-image. Perfectionism was emotionally crippling to me as a child, thwarting my spontaneity and freedom to make mistakes. I continue to suffer from perfectionism to this day, so deeply implanted is it in my brain, a no-win position. Dad yelled at us when we left lights on in unused rooms or left doors open, which let out precious heat, and he knew when we ran too much water in the bath. I kept my feelings to myself, but Jacquie argued with his rules.

At the same time, Dad was dignified and gracious, with a neatly trimmed mustache, thick white hair, classical nose and blue eyes, shielded by brown horn-rimmed glasses. He could be charming, especially when flirting with waitresses, nurses, or any female, often in front of Mum, who sloughed off his behavior saying, "Oh Tom, you are being silly!" Without her smooth diplomacy, our family would have suffered more quarrels instead of the seemingly endless silences, because Mum was generally unwilling or unable to assert herself. I wondered if she had been different before meeting Dad.

Mum loved Dad deeply and they had fun. Dad pulled her onto the floor, tickled her ribs and knees, while Mum writhed about and giggled, "Oh stop it, Tom, stop it!" Tom and Dolly were a loyal, devoted couple and throughout their fifty years of marriage, they never left the house without a kiss.

He was also a master of the Yorkshire put-down. "Mrs. Morley is a very pleasant lady, kind and not demanding, but I have to admit that she's no oil painting."

They shared a deep love of music. When Dad was young, he'd been a choir boy singing solos in church. He once took me to hear Handel's *Messiah*, his favorite oratorio, and I was amazed to see him in tears, deeply moved by the music and chorus. It was unfathomable to me, yet also encouraging, that such a stoic man could actually show that depth of emotion. Dad would shut his door whenever Jacquie or I practiced our scales and arpeggios, but would sit on the couch and listen for hours to Mum's lovely renditions of Chopin or Beethoven, and her *Clair de Lune* brought us all to tears. If we dared to speak, Dad whispered, "Shh — your mother is playing the piano."

He suffered severe bouts of bronchitis and emphysema. Despite the severity of his symptoms, he continued his smoking habit, deftly rolling his own cigarettes between his fingers. Mr. Trapp, who sold him Ritz papers and tobacco, used to say, "I'd never recognize your Dad without a cigarette in his mouth. Does he have a death wish, or what?"

Dad coughed and hacked and wheezed, especially in bitter weather. His ill health scared us and Mum often said wistfully, "I wish you would stop smoking, Tom."

"And give up my cough?" he chuckled.

Chapter 10

OLD RELIC

Dad chose old relics for his cars, defending his choices: "They are cheaper, sturdier, and I enjoy tinkering with them." Sunday trips to visit relatives across the Yorkshire moors were fraught with tension, initiated at home by Dad informing us that the old car had some mechanical problem. We were relieved to arrive at our destination, enjoying a "pleasant" lunch over banal chatter with relatives, Jacquie and I behaving properly to avoid trouble with Dad.

Before leaving our hosts, we filled our hot water bottles and Jacquie and I snuggled under the heavy brown rug in the back seat, dreading the trip home. Would we make it across the bleak, black, isolated Yorkshire moors? The fog was thick, visibility almost zero. But Dolly, Dad's nickname for Mum instead of Dorothy, saved us by heroically scrambling out of the car and slowly walking in the headlight beams, waving Dad's white handkerchief, and guiding our way through the treacherous fog.

Tensions mounted, but Dad sternly said, "Be quiet, and don't worry." However, the three of us, and probably Dad, too, were concerned, wondering if and when we would get home. Jacquie and I were cold, miserable, and wet, despite holding up a pan to catch the leaks from the dripping roof. But inevitably, we arrived home safely.

At night, under stacks of blankets, I squeezed the hot water bottle between my feet, even wearing protective bed socks. I awoke the next morning with burning chilblains on my toes, unable to tie up shoelaces because of painful swelling.

"Breakfast is ready!" yelled Mum as I lay in bed, fixated on the ice-covered window panes cracked into patterns like spiders' webs, warning me of the bitter temperature outside. But I eventually moved from my cozy cocoon.

Mum agonized that there would be no money for housekeeping. Dad always acquired the money, but teased poor Mum by pretending he was "out of funds." When he finally revealed the truth, Mum collapsed in relief.

Dad might have found the money needed to keep the household running, but there wasn't much left for other expenses. My tall, lanky body towered above my school friends, who had more attractive figures than mine. I was teased mercilessly, resulting in my hunched shoulders, eye contact with the floor, embarrassment and shame. I felt ugly. We had no money to buy new clothes, and Dad was too modest to ask for a raise at the company where he worked as a gas engineer. I wanted to shake him because his humility severely impacted the Coe's lifestyle. I was angry. Money ruled, being intricately connected with guilt and shame.

"I need new shoes. Mine have holes in the soles."

"We can't afford it. The school fees are due."

"PLEASE! I need new shoes! Send us to a public school."

"A superior education is worth all sacrifices," he'd state firmly. If we had known then that in his earlier years he'd worked in a coal mine and had taken engineering classes at night to gain an engineering degree, we might have better understood why hard work and education were two of his main values, which he had passed on to Jacquie and to me. But at the time private school just meant no new clothes, no vacations abroad, and no boys.

So life was one cold, stern struggle. *Skewed priorities*, I'd think angrily. I compared myself negatively to my school friends who could afford luxurious holidays in Europe, new clothes, swanky modern cars, televisions, and so on. I was jealous of their lifestyles.

I regularly tried to persuade Dad to buy a television, "All of my friends have TVs," but Dad refused, saying, "Television takes over a family and then your brains die."

I also loathed the rigid class system in the private school. Ears and eyes scrutinized my shoddy clothing, weather-beaten shoes, and Northern accent, to determine, "Is she in the low-middle or upper class—or in one of the subclasses? Are you worth getting to know?" This ruthless summation is shoved down one's throat the moment you pop into the world. My guts seethed for people to accept each other and to accept me.

Chapter 11

GREEN CARD

It was February 1965. My mailbox at the "Y" in London, where I had been living in order to work nearby, was crammed, including the long-awaited envelope from the Immigration Department. At last! The brown envelope, labeled with my name and address, had an immigration stamp at the corner. I was excited, but nervous about opening it. I held my breath, and ripped through the seal. The letter informed me that my green card, enabling me to work in California, would be in the mail by the end of April. I hollered with joy.

I had to keep busy to thwart my jitters as my departure day drew near. I finished my packing in my almost barren room at the Y, suddenly terrified about leaving the country. I didn't know anyone in California. Was I mad to leave my family and friends and all that was familiar to me?

My best friend, Sheila, threw a goodbye party for me in her flat, inviting our close friends. I feigned smiles of anticipated excitement, but felt crippled by nostalgia and fear of my unknown future. Would I ever see my friends again? Even if I did, how could our friendships remain the same?

"In thirty-six hours, you'll be at Heathrow ready to fly!" exclaimed Sheila, unaware of my anguish. My boyfriend, Peter, a cynical but witty architect, curly pipe always in his mouth, loved rock climbing, motor bikes, his old Austin

Healy, and me. He joined me sitting at the top of the stairs and offered me another pint of ale. I loved him, but not enough to get married, have children, plant flowers, and settle into a predictable, domestic life.

"Do you ever think about joining me in L.A?" I asked curiously.

"At least once a week," he replied. "But I don't have your courage, Annie." The beer nudged me further into grief. Suddenly I couldn't stop crying.

"Am I insane?" Tears dribbled into my beer. His hand tightened around mine.

"No, you are brave to follow your dream. Most of us drones are complacent. Playing it safe would be dangerous for you."

"But I'm frightened to death."

"I think you'll thrive in a new atmosphere. You're a survivor. And if you don't find what you want, you will come home. Nothing is written in stone."

"True," I said, half-heartedly. I wiped my eyes and cheeks with my sleeve, took a deep breath and polished off the beer. "Maybe one day I will actually find contentment. I yearn to recognize what I have and to feel satisfied with it. I hope L.A, in some way, can give me that."

A blustery wind whipped around Heathrow Airport. The sky was dark, threatening more rain. My mother, in a beret and tweed suit, appeared sad and worried, but kept reassuring me and herself that I was "level-headed and could look after myself."

But I knew she would worry — she always did. She lay in bed most nights worrying about everything, unable to stop, like an addict with no rehab programs available for recovery. Whenever Mum expressed her worries to Dad, he'd say in frustration, "Crikey Moses, Dolly! Stop that noddle of yours from all that work!" She'd feel rejected by his lack of compassion, but would say nothing.

Mum always depended on Dad to make decisions, leaving her powerless to fix things herself. In her female role as nurturer and protector, sometimes she would "help" by worrying about other peoples' problems as well as her own. Her face always appeared anxious and weary. I don't know how she managed on so little sleep.

My father, all decked out in his pink shirt and maroon cravat, was choked up, just as he had been at the *Messiah* performance. I was heartened again by his expression of emotion. Despite my ambivalent feelings towards Dad, I would miss his guidance, put-down humor, and even watching him roll his own cigarettes. I had always been convinced that his tobacco addiction would eventually lead to serious health issues, but here I was, about to leave my country, and missing Dad's habit for the first time ever.

"Lucky you! The sun and warmth will be waiting for you, but I'll miss pottering about London with you," said my sister, Jacquie. "I'll save up so I can visit you."

We clung to one another, probably the closest we had ever felt towards each other. The loudspeaker announced the final call for Pan Am flight 121. I was dizzy, palms wet and heart racing. We hurried to the side of the disappearing queue for last-minute photographs and good-byes. No longer able to cope with the emotional intensity, I grabbed my backpack and scrambled to the boarding area, where a cheeky cockney steward snatched my pass saying, "Get yer skates on, luv!" I glanced back but my family was hazy through the veil of my tears.

"Send us a telegram as soon as you arrive," my father hollered.

I stood there, glued to the spot, sniffling into my handkerchief. My lifelong dream beckoned, but waves of panic swept over me. Shall I go back? I was mad for abandoning the love of my family and friends. The steward intervened in my dilemma.

"Let's go, luv. No time for stragglers. The hatch is about to close."

I forced myself through the gate and burst into tears. I sank into my seat by the window, feeling in limbo, scared, but now on my way to another life. The engines were on, I watched the stewardesses showing off safety precautions, but I didn't listen.

"No man is an island," wrote the poet John Donne. But I was an island, always apart, never with the group. An alien dropped onto earth with an omnipresent and niggling restlessness that screamed for some peace so that, for once, I could be acquainted with that strange phenomenon called *contentment.*

Maybe in California I wouldn't feel alienated, maybe I would feel more a part of life. Please let me not be disappointed. I wanted to find a real home.

Chapter 12

ARRIVAL

I arrived in Los Angeles on June 22nd, 1965, and spent my first night at a "Hotel Flamingo" on Ocean Avenue, directly across from the Santa Monica beach. My sleep had been erratic, my physical and emotional clocks being in a state of surreal disconnection. It was 6:30 a.m. Despite my initial disorientation, I grasped for shorts and a tee-shirt, excited that within a few minutes I would finally laze on a California beach. I was careful to cross the busy street called Pacific Avenue with all that traffic going the "wrong way."

I squinted in the intense sunlight and saw my first glimpse of the blue-green Pacific Ocean, reveling in the deep, fine sand which swallowed up my feet. A white beach as far as the eye could see.

Back in England, pebbled beaches were more prevalent. You usually had to dress in layers, wooly scarves, even gloves, and solid rubber sandals such as skin divers wore. Now, I would buy myself bikinis and sunglasses.

I stretched out on my beach towel, admiring the infinite span of ocean, glistening far out to the horizon, and the Santa Monica Mountains in the background, dotted with Spanish-style mansions decorated with bougainvillea in various shades of orange, scarlet and fuchsia. I had dreamed of this moment for years. I was finally here! California! I lay there dozing amidst the intoxicating sounds of the waves lapping and gulls crying out. Paradise!

As the morning hours passed, the sun became brighter and hotter, warming my skin. I was caressed by gentle wisps of wind. Eventually, I heard distant voices of people visiting the beach. As their voices approached, I tuned into a chorus of high-pitched British accents. Was I hallucinating? Was this the result of jet lag? I sat up in shock and discovered Brits all around me. I was dumbfounded. I had travelled six thousand miles to be with Americans, not Brits!

Later, I learned from the hotel manager that Santa Monica boasted a large English community, catering to it with pubs, tea shops, and stores laden with British goods. Despite the beach lifestyle, I decided that this was not where I wanted to live, even though I liked British people. My plan had always been to fully experience America and the American way of life.

When the Santa Ana hot winds are blowing through L.A., one can see as far as the eyes will allow. The Hollywood sign seems to sparkle from almost any area of the city. It is a seductive sight, symbolizing the lure and excitement of the entertainment business.

Despite missing my family and friends in England, I didn't miss the rigid class system, nasty weather, and the abundant limitations of living there. I continue, to this day, to be grateful for listening to my instincts and following my dream.

That was the first time it had ever occurred to me to ask myself, "What exactly *is* my dream?

All of my energy up to now had been devoted to leaving England and my immigration to California, getting a place to live, and settling in. Nothing else had been important. It wasn't until I got to Los Angeles that it dawned on me that I needed to start thinking about a career. How I envied all those people who had identified the career they wanted by the age of nine, and pursued it. I remember reading a quote from Barbra Streisand, "You have got to discover you, what you do, and trust it."

I wanted to find my niche and acquire the necessary education and experience to become a successful professional — at *something*. I just didn't know yet what that something was.

In the meantime I had to start somewhere to bring in some money as I was making up my mind, so I answered a want ad for a secretarial position at a hospital working for three doctors involved in cancer research. Three *urologists*. It was so *un*glamorous, so *un*Hollywood, that I was embarrassed to answer when people asked me cheerily, "So Annie, tell us what *you* do?"

I work for three urologists.

Chapter 13

A DOG

On my regular walks around my neighborhood, I started seeing a neglected champagne-colored terrier wandering aimlessly all over the road, or sleeping around the base of palm trees on Russell Avenue. After three days of these heartbreaking visions, I searched for him, a welcome distraction from the necessity of looking for another job that I could think of as a career, or at least leading *into* a career. Finally, I saw the dog, limping along the pavement without tags. He was so starved and zonked that he allowed me to check him out. Matted hair. Ribs protruding. He sank down at my feet, panting, forlorn gooey eyes pleading for attention. "Please, please save me and take care of me."

How could I not take this heartbroken creature home and at least feed him? I took off my sweatshirt to wrap him in my arms, for both of our safety's sake. I smuggled him into my apartment where he lapped up a large bowl of water before conking out in an exhausted sleep. The cats hid in a closet, sensing the potential danger nearby. Magic and Dickens emerged cautiously, sniffed around him, and, then, unthreatened, retreated to their favorite ray of sunshine in the bedroom.

My career preoccupation had been replaced by this sweet, homeless pup. An animal shelter was out of the question, as they were renowned for euthanizing strays brought in without tags. After three days, I stapled "Lost Dog" fliers onto telephone poles and palm tree trunks, over several blocks. I spent hours calling pet shops, veterinary hospitals, lost animal agencies, adoption foundations, but no one would guarantee a home or medical help for him.

Meanwhile, "Jake," as I christened him, continued to scarf down food and enjoy his walks with me (on a piece of sturdy string from my "fix-it drawer"), his tail coming up to half mast. Magic and Dickens gradually became more interested in him as each day passed.

I cautiously approached the landlady of the building in apartment five. She was a behind-the-curtain watcher, always snooping on her tenants. She must have seen everyone who came and went. Not surprisingly, the door opened before I knocked.

"What do you want at this time of the morning?" she snarled. "Is it about that barking dog you smuggled in? He has to go, now."

"Look at him, for heaven's sake. He's starved, sick..."

"One week, or I set him free myself." I couldn't do anything other than blink as she rudely slammed the door in my face. An instant later, she opened it again, saying menacingly, "He'd better not make any mess. You'll be liable, you know." She slammed the door again.

"I'll find a place!" I shouted. "Bitch," I muttered under my breath. I made relentless calls to apartments, always greeted with "No pets allowed." I was desperate. Magic Kelly, Charlie Dickens, Jake and I had to remain a family. Jake fawned after a pristine grooming, with fluffy hair and a full tummy. I wondered if he had ever felt so comfortable and loved.

Finally, my eyes scanned the UCLA *Bruin* newspaper which offered hope in the form of an ad. I checked out an art deco, three story house, nestled in the hills, which had a room for rent on the lower level. The room was cozy, wood-paneled, and led to a small yard with a Meyer lemon tree laden with fruit close by the windows. The fragrance permeated the room. There was a swimming pool surrounded by wild growths of crimson bougainvillea which climbed around the high edges on the top level, by the street. A huge living and dining room overlooked the vastness of Los Angeles.

The separate quarters for seven (soon to include me) housed a cinematographer, a lawyer with his two whippets, a teacher/artist, a gym trainer, a teacher, and an accountant. They were an eclectic group who had established house rules and policies several years ago. I passed their interview, and moved in a month later with Jake, Magic, and Dickens.

Inspired by burning sunrises and sunsets, I walked the hills and chatted with mostly artistic neighbors, while Jake teased their dogs' snouts under curly wrought iron gates. I had fun living there. The seven of us embraced each other's individuality, learning about acceptance and compassion while ironing out our conflicts. We prepared weekly dinners to *The Big Chill* soundtrack, dancing about with plates and playing catch with oranges. To be alone or to join in with the group was the best of both worlds. The roommates often brought intriguing characters to visit the house, like Chevy Chase, Burt Lancaster, Stephen Stills, musicians and singers and poets and screenwriters.

Wine bottles clanking in knapsacks, my roommates and I would trundle down the rickety wooden staircase to Highland Avenue, and then on to the Hollywood Bowl to hear outdoor classical music concerts, and performances by such artists as Benny Goodman, Ravi Shankar and the Moody Blues. Up to twenty-five thousand people ate gourmet pasta and popped champagne corks in the open air, an old tradition, while waiting for the concert to begin. Adding to the atmosphere were the stars, picnic baskets and flickering candles, and the sounds of crickets and distant planes. It was electric!

I could have gone on like this forever, but the time finally came when I knew I'd have to think about what I wanted to be when I grew up. I still needed to find my mission in life lest I go batty with boredom with my three urologists. I had a job; I wanted a career.

Chapter 14

SCHOOLED

My dad had always stressed education, and after being in America for a while, I realized that my education didn't have to be over. It could continue for as long as I wished on any subject I wished. That came as something of a revelation.

For example, my ignorance of the U.S. political system brought up those familiar old feelings of inferiority, but at first I comforted myself with the thought that I was still an immigrant, not a citizen, though my application sat among thousands of others at the Immigration Department. I knew I was smart, just un-informed, so I decided to attend Los Angeles City College (LACC) where I registered for a class in political science.

It was motivating to walk up the campus steps, and enter the red brick building which swarmed with students of all ages and ethnicities, hurrying about with books and files under their arms, or lazing about on the lawns until the bell rung for class.

I loved being a schoolgirl again, and loved feeling I was finally getting educated. As soon as one class was over, I'd sign up for another. After two years of this, I earned my A.A. Degree. I immediately switched to another college where I began to work on my B.A. degree, all the while still working for my three urologists to pay the bills.

Even though I was enjoying my classes, and enjoying an active social life with friends, including male friends — and even though finding a brilliant career was still an unresolved problem and much on my mind — I was also yearning for something else. I was yearning to be in a relationship. I had been alone now for several years. My friends and co-workers at the lab all knew that I was on the lookout; I was active in the Chamber of Commerce and attended community affairs and meetings, yet I had never met a man I wanted to date. I wanted that connection and spark that comes with a mature relationship that actually works, rather than act as someone's mother or live-in babysitter. I wanted love.

Chapter 15

KIT

I met Betsy Thompson in a public speaking class. Lively, sweet, with twinkly eyes, her demeanor and charm and curiosity reminded me of my dear Mum with her short, white cropped hair. Later, I was astonished to learn that she was thirty years older than I. Despite our age difference, we became close friends, supporting each other through our anxieties about our speeches, grades, and personal lives.

One evening she invited me to a performance of *Don Quixote* at the college theater. I agreed to join her, but on this particular night my mind was elsewhere, still struggling with the puzzle of my life's mission. Yes, I was working for my college degree, but once I had it, what then?

The first act of the play explored the comical and provocative relationship between the idealist dreamer, Quixote, and his squire, Sancho, a materialistic realist. I became engrossed in the witty dialogues, forgetting most of my worries. The audience broke into exuberant applause as the curtain closed for intermission.

We maneuvered up the crowded aisles into the foyer, gabbing about the play's eloquent writing and talented actors, when suddenly Betsy waved at a tall, striking young man across the room whose commanding presence seemed to effortlessly take over the room.

He reminded me of a dark-haired Peter O'Toole. She led me over to him, and brought our arms together, proudly saying, "Annie, this is my son, Christopher."

"Your son?!" I muttered, shocked at this Adonis.

"I am very pleased to meet you," he said eagerly.

I was shaken by waves of vulnerability as he placed his big palm into mine, offering an open smile and steady gaze. He must have been six feet four inches, muscular but slender with piercing brown eyes. His dark looks were accentuated by a long-sleeved black turtleneck, black cords, and worn brown cowboy boots. He was the most handsome and charismatic man I had ever met. My eyes strayed from his for an instant to the violet and green splotches on his fingers.

He responded to the flick of my eyes, "I'm a painter."

I nodded with a smile, continuing to be unbalanced by his presence.

Noticing my unusual silence, Betsy chirped in, "Christopher- Kit- lived in Venice Beach, but thankfully moved west to Hollywood."

I wondered why "thankfully" but couldn't bring myself to speak, stunned by his presence. My cheeks were flushed and my mouth felt dry. My mind told me to be wise and self-protective, and to control the churning inside me.

Go to the W.C. to sort yourself out, I told myself. But I couldn't. My feet were glued to the floor. I simply yearned for this man to sweep me up in his long arms and fly away with me. It was as though he had known me for all time. I had never felt anything remotely like that in my life.

Before the lights dimmed for Act II, Betsy leaned over to whisper, "I gave him your phone number. I hope you don't mind."

I was miffed. "Why didn't you ask me first?"

"I should have. I'm sorry," she answered as the curtain opened. I patted her arm, unable to speak as the next part of the performance began.

She was matchmaking! Surely her son had hordes of girlfriends. Idealistic visions circled my mind for the first time in years. Since I had been about eight years old, I had dreamed that my "prince" would suddenly appear before me, but I discarded this notion long after many disappointments in my relationships with men, mostly Peter Pans.

My mind scattered about, unable to concentrate on the second act. I was conflicted as to whether I should ask Betty about her son, but I sensed that it would be wiser to learn about Kit myself, since information from others could easily skew the truth.

During the next several days, I felt like a teenager, obsessing about him, waiting, waiting for my phone to ring. If he did call, would I see him or not? I wondered why the mere ten minutes of Kit's presence moved me to such an unknown depth of feelings. I was scared, not understanding my intense emotional reaction. Dad's words chimed into my head. *Pull yourself together, Annie.*

He was right. I needed to think. If Kit did call, maybe I'd see him. Maybe not. If he didn't call, I would return to emotional safety, my dithers would stop, and I would continue to embrace my rich L.A. life. For the first time since I'd left home, I realized that I liked the power of control and independence. It was not in my nature to simply wait.

Two nights later, my phone rang. It was Kit. I kept my voice steady.

"I'd like to see you again," he said eagerly.

Without hesitation, I answered, "Me, too."

"I take my dog for an early walk along the Griffith Park trails when the light is changing. How about tomorrow?"

"Great. Can I bring Jake, my well-behaved mutt?"

"Will you pick me up? I am unable to drive right now because of a DUI."

An imposing red flag floated across my vision. I wondered if Kit were an alcoholic. But I ignored my questions and wrote down his address, arranging to meet him at nine the next morning, a Monday. I replaced the receiver, leaping with childish glee inside, thankful I had taken a week off work to catch up with my studies. I would ask him about the DUI tomorrow.

8 a.m. at last, time to drive to West Hollywood. More tall and handsome than I had remembered, Kit stood outside his studio with Eddie, his family's black and brown mutt.

"Hello, Annie," he said with that all-embracing smile of his. I had never felt such a powerful physical attraction before, and had to stop myself from hugging him or even touching his arm. My decision had been to be cautious and simply gather information about him.

He let Eddie jump into the back with Jake, then sank into the seat next to me.

"You move like a cat, smooth and slinky," I remarked.

"Thanks," he grinned, "but I frequently bump into things or lose my balance, and yet my sisters still call me 'Kitten!'" He laughed and soothed the dogs as they sniffed each other out in the back.

I drove along Franklin Avenue, then north on Vermont into the park.

"Look!" Kit exclaimed, pointing at the sun's rays filtering through the stately fir trees. "Let's park by this trail so we won't miss the morning colors."

I delighted in his enthusiasm as I slid into a parking space, no other cars in sight. We were by ourselves. Children were in school, people were busy at work, and only an occasional Parks and Recreation worker tended the grounds. The distant sound of a helicopter and police siren interrupted the silence.

Crisp air on my face.

"Brr..." I shivered, buttoning up my jacket, secretly hoping Kit would warm me with a hug. I knew that he knew what I had hinted for, and I felt annoyed with myself having done so, but he made no comment or move toward me.

Jake and Eddie bounded away up the trail, leaving us to honor the beauty around us, with dramatic views of the Planetarium, Hollywood sign and hills.

"Let's move on while the sun remains low," Kit said as we walked on in the direction of where the dogs were sniffing around. The occasional brush of a leaf against my face. Sensual. He aroused my senses and he knew it. I blushed. He had an uncanny ability to thrill me and yet calm me at the same time.

"England. Do you miss it?"

"At the risk of sounding shallow, England is rich in architectural beauty and heritage, but the sun and free lifestyle here have fed me in a profound way. When I was growing up, the class system was rigid and I wanted out of it. Not to mention the foul weather."

"You were brave to come here alone."

That he'd even considered that touched me deeply.

Kit's knowledge and love of nature intrigued me. In few words, he poetically spoke about the undulations of the hills, the movement and layers of the cumulus clouds, and the pungent fragrances around us. He snapped off twigs of sage and rosemary, bay, and eucalyptus leaves, and an abundance of others, foreign smells to me, and asked me to close my eyes to describe the myriad of scents.

We stopped at a clearing with unblocked vistas of the hills. He pointed out the intricate interplays between the light and shadows, what was real and what was illusion. He then described all the shades of color.

"To truly see and know what is real is a lifelong struggle."

To be around someone so alive was intoxicating.

As we drove down the hill, Kit asked, "Would you like to do this again? There are many trails to take and wondrous sights to behold."

"I'd love it," I replied, curbing the excitement within me. There had been nothing ordinary about these two hours.

"Would you mind if we left the dogs at home? They're distracting."

"Good idea. I am free each morning this week."

As we approached his studio, Kit said, "How about Thursday morning, same time?"

I smiled and nodded.

"I must paint now."

"What are you working on?"

"A portrait of a friend. It's a commission. Not much money for all the time I've spent on it, but it is the only way I can make some kind of a living right now. C'mon Eddie…"

Kit waved me off. I'd ask him about his DUI next time, I told myself as I drove off, knowing my life had changed in some way. My mind wandered to thoughts about Kit. Nobody had ever provoked fear in me as he had, unleashing a depth of emotion, which somehow I had to tame. I was chuffed with myself for holding back, not barging in with loads of questions, trying to impress him or gain his approval. But thoughts about him continued to swirl around my head. I wondered if he had a girlfriend, or many, if he had talent. I hoped to see his studio soon, which would give me more information.

Stop, Annie, stop! I scolded myself, not liking the feeling of being ungrounded, so when I got home I forced myself to sit outside in the yard on my redwood bench under the lemon tree while I tried to clear my mind.

Thursday morning. One of my roommates, Janet, hurried in to grab a banana and leave for her teaching job. "What's happening, Annie? You have a new glow in those English cheeks of yours."

I beamed. "I have a crush!"

"What's he like in bed?"

I chuckled in admiration at Janet's boldness to go directly to the heart of things. Her hobbies were men, sex, writing, music and poetry, and smoking pot.

"I have no idea," I giggled self-consciously.

"I hope you find out soon!" She grabbed her briefcase and blew me a kiss as she rushed out the door.

My telephone rang. It was only 6:30 a.m. A wrong number? Kit? Yes, Kit. Slurring his speech, difficult to understand.

"I-can't-go-for-a-walk. I'll call you."

Click.

He was drunk or hung over. Tears welled up in my eyes. I left my tea on the counter, dragged myself downstairs, let Jake out into the yard and crawled back into bed, throwing the comforter over my head to hide from my disappointment. *You lost yourself in dreamland, wearing rose-tinted glasses. It's all your own fault.*

That night, I decided to call Kit to relieve some of my pent- up feelings. Barbra Streisand said, "It is every woman's dream to be some man's dream woman." But not like this. I took a deep breath and dialed his number. He answered on the third ring.

"What happened to our second walk in the park? Where were you?"

"Uhhh, sorry. I screwed up. I got smashed the night before," he replied sheepishly.

"I was mad at you. I don't like being stood up. And now I wonder about you and alcohol, your DUI..."

"Sometimes my demons overwhelm me and off I go to the liquor store to numb myself. I feel wretched and hate myself the next day, unable to function, let alone paint. It's a futile cycle because the demons always return."

I had a sense of despair listening to him. A haunted soul, so opposite from what I had learned about him previously. "What demons?"

"They've plagued me all my life," he admitted. "Will I ever find peace from my monster father who used to drink and pummel us five times a day? Will I ever make enough money to survive as an artist? How can I belong in this mundane world?"

Despite my disappointment, I tried to buck him up, even though I wanted to question him further. There I went again, honoring him before myself. "You seem to feel at home in nature."

"Trips into nature are temporary. I cannot go and hide in the wilds. Only in my imagination can I visit lands that offer comfort and inspiration."

I shuddered. My eyes were wet. "I want a friendship with you, Kit. But not with you and booze. It's too dramatic."

"All I can say is that I'm working on it. Alcohol is toxic to me."

Despite my warning signs about Kit, I saw him several times over the next few weeks. He saw where I lived, met my roommates, and we asked endless questions about each other's lives. We were becoming more intimate.

He usually carried a sketchbook, drawing detailed pictures of me wherever we were, or writing stories and poetry while I studied. He stimulated my mind and my senses; our conversations were never ordinary.

We explored the beach areas, Vasquez Rocks, the Santa Monica and San Gabriel Mountains and the Pacific Coast, all areas I thought I knew, but with Kit, I experienced them as I never had before.

He awoke my senses, my heart; I had never felt so alive. We hiked up the side and behind the Hollywood sign, gazing up at the gleaming white letters high above us.

"In the twenties, the sign said 'Hollywoodland' which was a real estate company at that time," Kit said. "Apparently, at night it was brilliantly lit by thousands of bulbs. It must have been a magical sight. Sadly, vandals smashed the bulbs, ending that history."

Not thinking and as usual, moved by being in his presence, I started to embrace him, but he gently guided my arms down by my side.

"I want you to know, Annie," he said earnestly, "that for years, girls have been 'after me,' not for who I am, but for how I look, or the romantic idea of my being an artist. I was flattered, but I could never trust them. They wanted to have sex without our knowing anything about each other. Empty and unfulfilled. It's not worth it. So I don't."

"It's not about me?"

"No, Annie. I want time to pass to build our friendship and trust for each other."

"I suppose you're wise," I uttered, disappointment in my heart. I changed the subject to ease the tension in the air, just like my mother.

"Why did your mother want you to move from Venice Beach?"

"I hung out with characters who did nothing but get drunk and stoned — and I did the same thing for almost a year, crashing on the beach or somebody's couch. I was dying. Mom lent me money so I could move up here to draw and paint, which I was born to do. I don't want to be a pathetic drunk like my monster parent."

"Then you won't be."

"It's a daily struggle."

I wanted to find out more, but he changed the subject.

On Malibu beach one sunny, hot southern California afternoon, Kit sat bare-chested at his easel, and I sat in a beach chair, drafting out a paper on my interpretation for *Waiting for Godot* by Samuel Beckett for my course on existential writers. Several families played in the sand nearby. Every so often, Kit put down his palette and brush, sprinted across the blistering sand to the sea, diving into the waves, swimming far away until he was a mere dot on the horizon.

He was drawn to the water, always diving into swimming pools, rivers, lakes, the sea, in whatever weather, or however dark the night. A few weeks ago, we had spent the day wandering around Laguna Beach, in and out of unimpressive art galleries, and enjoying a seafood lunch with a view over the Pacific.

Another time at midnight, when we were smooching on Laguna Beach, he suddenly leapt up, stripped naked, and ran into the ocean, arms flailing about in joy like a child. The moonlight helped me spot him for a while. Then he vanished. I held my breath in fear. Silence. Ten minutes passed; surely it had been an hour. I got up from the blanket, bare feet on cold sand, and breathed deeply, trying to ease my anxiety.

I couldn't see anyone on the beach. What could I do?

At last! There he was! Glowing, dripping, and hollering in rejuvenation. I, on the other hand, was on the edge of a panic attack.

"You terrify me, Christopher Thompson! You're a daredevil! Aren't you ever scared?"

"No! I am reborn!"

At the end of one painting day, he showed me his work. Its realism startled me... the sand pockets, the gentle river flowing down from the hillside behind us, the curls of the waves, and in the background, filing across the bridge behind us, about a half a mile away, were four magnificent elephants following each other. I was astounded. How had he conjured up such a startling image? I was transported.

"The colors flow through my brush more easily with you next to me."

I beamed at his compliment. "Why did you paint the elephants?"

"The vision came to me. They lift the picture into mysterious, otherworldly realms."

We arrived back at Kit's after a blissful drive down the Pacific Coast Highway, serenaded by scarlet, crimsons and purples of the darkening sky.

"Would you like to come in?" he asked, unexpectedly. I tried to curb my excitement. He usually said, "I'll see you soon."

I turned off the motor. We unpacked the car and I followed him into a tightly packed room which served as his studio, living room and bedroom. Rolls of canvas and pieces of wood leaned against one wall. Several easels, boxes crammed with paint tubes and brush sets, some in jars of liquid, were in a corner next to his couch, which served as a bed, surrounded by drawings, clippings, and photos. On one wall was a door, to the loo, I thought, and a shelf stocked with a hot plate, cans of food and cereal boxes. Several burger wrappers were scattered about. A strong odor of oil paint, and something like turpentine, permeated the room.

Two unfinished portraits and many photographs were pinned up on every available space. I thought about my years of restlessness and all those years in England, trying to provoke people to be authentic — what did they really think and feel underneath all that pleasant chatter? Kit's quest was constant and more profound, managing to seek the soul of his subjects.

"Your artist's lair, bang in the midst of West Hollywood. I like it," I said. He handed me a Coke and sat close to me on the couch. I tried to ignore my increasing pulse.

"Did you make those?" I asked, pointing to a cardboard geodesic dome, a cube and a triangle, about eight to ten inches tall, surrounded by tubes of glue, a compass, pencil, and watercolor paint set.

"They're for a still-life I want to do. I like to work from reality, not photos or what I just *imagine* is true."

"Your interests are eclectic," I said, swigging from the bottle as I scanned the titles of books he had piled on the floor. "Astronomy, biology, world history, poetry, artists... who is your favorite artist?"

A quiet lulled between us. I could hear my heart beating. He gently moved some hair from my eyes, drew my face to his, and kissed me again and again. My forehead, cheeks, nose, ears and to my lips, less tender now. I shivered all over with a primitive hunger. He started to unbutton my blouse. My heart jack-hammered in my chest as we began to make love.

On a sweltering July afternoon, shielded by sunglasses and caps, we dripped our way west on the Santa Monica Freeway and through the McClure Tunnel, at the end of which we were greeted by a glistening vista of the Pacific, and miles and miles of white sand, a sight which always excites me. We sang along with *The Doors* amidst the traffic, speeding by flashy convertibles with bare arms waving. I waved in glee at a couple in a pristine E-type silver Jaguar, the one with the sexy, long bonnet, the radio blaring out *Fun, Fun, Fun.*

"The Beach Boys!" I said as we sped by the Jag. "I played their songs over and over at the "Y" in London, yearning to live in California. When I was fifteen, my dad— although I had to suffer through his impatience—taught me to drive in a Mark XII Jag on the runways of a deserted American Air Force base, and Jags have been my favorite cars ever since. I got my license first test out and swore that one day, I would be the proud owner of a Jag. They're sexy and classy."

"You'll have your Jag," Kit said knowingly. "You're the only person I ever met who achieves your goals."

I so desperately wanted Kit to achieve his goal that I decided to introduce him to a London art gallery owner I'd met at a New Year's Eve party at his estate in the Thames Valley — - and now he was visiting in Los Angeles. I insisted that Kit bring his paints. He resisted. I insisted.

"I'm excited to see Anthony again," I exclaimed.

"Why, did you have an affair with him?"

Chuffed by Kit's tinge of jealousy, I pinched him on the butt and sloppily kissed him on the back of his neck just as we arrived at the party.

"It's about time you showed up," Anthony said to me at the door with a hug. "And you must be Kit."

Within moments the two men soared into animated conversation, instant friends. Anthony asked Kit to paint a portrait of him right then and there, next to the pool full of bikini babes. Kit set up and got to work.

"All I ask is that you hold still," said Kit.

"I could be lining up a dolly for tonight. How much longer do you require my attention?"

After half an hour, sensitive to Anthony's plight and overall fidgitiness, Kit grinned, "You're done! I can detail it without you. Time for you to dolly-spot!"

Anthony popped open another beer and slurped it down before moving around the easel for a view. My mind was spinning. Would he like the painting? *Please let Anthony be the lead we were looking for, please!*

Through Anthony's raucous laugh, he exclaimed, "You've captured an uncanny resemblance to me, even my squint. You vagabond!" he said, hugging Kit boisterously.

Kit calmly cleaned off his palette and brushes. I leapt with joy within myself at the portrait's success, knowing that Anthony never said anything he didn't mean.

"Let's go down to the beach," said Kit, stretching his stiff arms and back after painting. We jumped over the wall, down the grassy embankment and onto the sand. A strong embrace before Kit ran off and dove into the sea, his long arms knifing the waves in a backstroke, until he eventually returned to the wet sand, and flopped down to rest.

I continued to feel in awe of this man who taught me so much about life every day. I would write down his wise words, such as, "Never allow people to influence who you are, then no one can ever take you away from you." "The love I hold for you, Anne, I shall hold for all time." "Never do I make a move, but it is colored by your presence... Art is a revelation of love."

Kit was an "old soul," never ceasing to amaze me. I knew I wanted to be by his side for the rest of my life.

Anthony not only wanted to buy the painting Kit had just done, but he then offered Kit a commission to paint Elijah being drawn up in a fiery chariot from the River Jordan, driven by eight horses into the kingdom of heaven. This would be painted on a large canvas, five feet by seven feet. Kit promised that with mathematics and careful drawings, and painting as far as possible from reality, he could complete the commission within three months. The painting would be showcased in Anthony's art gallery in central London. And this offer, after seeing only the portrait of Anthony — with a substantial down payment.

A break at last. We were jubilant!

Kit bought new oil paints and stretch bars to assemble the canvas. He was highly motivated, excited when I was able to be by his side. He spent any available free time drawing horses, either on the horse trails in Griffith Park, the Equestrian Center, or Beachwood Stables. He struggled to capture the majestic animals in motion, the form of their legs, flanks, body muscles, his sketching becoming more detailed.

About one month later, Kit completed a huge, detailed sketch of the painting to be created, which he Xeroxed in parts for Anthony, who was then back in England. The commission and possibilities of future creative and financial successes lifted Kit's mood into new heights, as he had lived as a struggling painter for so long. And to us, as a couple, it promised a more exciting, more stable future. Our plans to marry the following year became more real. Because of Anthony's generous down payment, we were relieved not to continue to scrap about in order to pay for meals and incidentals.

Kit arranged to drive up to the Kern River in Bakersfield, to paint the "River Jordan" from the Kern. He would stay by the river, in the same area where we had camped together about nine months earlier. I was disappointed that my work in the path lab and my classes in college prevented me from going with him. He left early that Monday morning.

"I'll call you by Wednesday," he said. "I will miss you. Thank you for all that you do for me. I love you." He kissed my cheek again, and was gone.

Wednesday. No call from Kit. No call by late night on Wednesday. I started to feel highly anxious. The next morning I decided to drive up there.

I found his car stripped, the convertible top strewn on the ground, all slashed up and muddied, ghostly skulls and cross bones drawn over the dash. I couldn't breathe. I thought something terrible had occurred. From a nearby roadside phone, I blurted the story to a forest ranger.

Helicopters circled above. I screeched to a halt and parked above where we had camped together, huge boulders surrounding river pools below the steep embankment.

I saw a body, face down, on the surface of one of the pools. Blue and bloated. I started screaming and screaming, stumbling and falling down the rocky hillside, shrieking and crying and yelling, "No, no, no, no... NOOOO!"

Before I knew it, a sheriff's chest was in front of me, trying to hold down my arms as I beat on his chest, again and again, with a herculean force, bloodying my fingers as I hit the points of his badge, bellowing and howling, still trying to beat his chest, my wailing echoing in the otherwise quiet canyon. The sheriff managed to control my flailing, his arms around me as I wailed and sobbed into his chest. I wanted to die.

After a while, the sheriff helped me up the embankment, but I kept collapsing. He was kind and patient. The coroner asked if I wanted to identify the body. I couldn't.

My life changed forever. Just as it had when I first met Christopher Thompson.

Despite the posters offering descriptions of missing items and money rewards, the Mamiya camera I had lent Kit was never found, nor were his easel, paints, sketch pads, the large drawing of his commission.

The final report by the coroner's office described no foul play. Christopher had dived into the pool, probably in twilight, when elusive shadows and light dance in the water. About a foot below the surface, Kit's head hit a mossy ledge, which instantly broke his neck.

My lover, soulmate, fiancé, genius, dead at the age of twenty-seven.

Chapter 16

A HOLLYWOOD PARTY

Grief owned me for more than two years after Kit's death. The fact that I was still working in the private practice office of the three urologists turned out to be a blessing in disguise because it was a low-stress job, very routine, which is about all I could handle emotionally. I had also continued with school, getting my BA degree in English Literature. But mostly I holed up and secluded myself.

Then in March of 1974, I got an invitation to a Hollywood party, a refreshing change from parties full of hospital lab techs. Dressed to the nines and driving my old MG, I headed for the address in an ivy-covered, two-story apartment complex in Hollywood, on a street lined with stocky palm trees, their fronds swaying high above the brick wall that curled around a central swimming pool. I continued to remain enchanted with these typical L.A sights even though I had already been living here for several years.

I was greeted by the host, Scotty, from a class I'd taken on Shakespeare. He was all smiles and hugs, more gay than usual here in his own environment, and nattily dressed in Cargo shorts and a stylish Hawaiian flower shirt. He took my hand and started introducing me to his friends, most of them deeply engaged in conversations about the movie business.

"What do you do, Annie?"

"I work in the office of three doctors."

"What kind of doctors?"

"Urologists," I said, knowing the reaction I'd get.

"Ah."

Despite Scotty's kind efforts to encourage conversation, I felt very much alone at the party, a fish out of water. Was I the only person there with a *real* job? Scotty finally wandered away.

Yes, I was a nine-to-fiver with a stable and predictable job which had served its purpose for the last two years, but my lack of enthusiasm had been gnawing at me lately. I wanted to feel alive again, that way I had felt with Kit. Why else had I moved to L.A. from London in the first place — but to feel alive and free? Instead, I had become a clock-watcher, waiting for the long days to end so I could go home for a swim. But boredom is like a slow death, and the longer it goes on, the harder it is to motive oneself to make a change.

A willowy blond in a mid-calf lace and satin dress, black suede granny boots and strings of pearls waved me over. She looked impatient to be rescued from the young man flanking her side, firing questions at her about how to succeed in the entertainment business.

"You have to be a real pest, bug those in power to remember you," she was saying as I walked up to them. "Send photos to everyone, call your agent daily, read the trades, and contact anyone on the crew or a film in production."

"And what, Carolyn, get the big brush-off?"

She gladly interrupted him to introduce me. "This is..."

"Annie," I said. I knew she had no idea who I was. "I'm an acquaintance of Robert."

"Annie agrees with me, I'm sure."

"It sounds like good advice," I said.

"You're English," Carolyn said.

"I know." We both laughed.

She turned back to the young wanna-be. "I know of a production assistant position open, if you're interested in that," she offered.

"No way!" he replied, indignantly. "I'm an actor! I don't want to make coffee for anyone!"

I jumped in. "I would think that depends on who you are making coffee *for.*"

I met Carolyn's gaze, sharing a moment with her. *This is L.A. If he's not willing to work an entry-level job, Hollywood will swallow him whole.*

Grinning, Carolyn shook my hand, while the young actor stalked inside for another Mai-Tai.

On impulse, I said, "*I'm* interested! Will you please tell me about it?" I startled myself: *what was I saying?* I was a lunatic to even think I would leave my urologists for the stress of show business. I had no knowledge about filmmaking. I was speechless and dizzy, or was it the Mai-Tais?

She flashed a lovely smile and explained that my first interview would be with a Spanish producer, André, working out of Samuel Goldwyn Studios. She scribbled a phone number on a napkin and handed it to me.

"Call him. And call him back if he doesn't respond." She tossed her hair back. "By the way, the job is working for Orson Welles."

An adrenaline rush gripped me the moment I heard the name of the famous filmmaker, Orson Welles. But that was the extent of my knowledge—that he was a famous filmmaker.

Chapter 17

THE INTERVIEW

The Spanish producer, André, was dark, with an olive complexion and intense eyes. His slight frame was draped in an impeccably tailored black suit with a cobalt blue silk cravat tucked neatly into his shirt. The walls of his office were covered with posters, photos, and clippings of Orson Welles and his movies. André stood behind a huge mahogany desk piled with papers and scripts arranged in neat, straight lines. He swept away his stubborn black locks to ogle me as I sank into the cushy chair opposite him, wriggling to pull down my skirt.

He ignored the ringing phones to pour on the charm. It fell dead on me. In seeming disbelief at my lack of response to him, he abruptly switched into a business-like mode and told me to meet Orson at noon sharp the next day at his suite in the Century Plaza Hotel.

He thrust a card in my hand and picked up the phone, my cue to leave. As an afterthought, and with an air of nonchalance, he questioned my film and television qualifications. My stomach sank. I blushed and stammered, glossing over several fictional movie jobs I had "worked" on in London — titles I had created on the drive over.

"But now," I said, intending to extricate myself from my lie, "I work at USC Medical Center with three doctors on a cancer research project."

He dialed his phone and muttered, "Good luck."

I quickly closed the door behind me and fled to my pathetic little car, rising above its shabbiness to wave professionally at the studio gate guard as I sped away in the direction of the Hollywood sign, which never failed to conjure up magical images in my mind of movies and stardom. My churning stomach drew me back to the interview, which was superficial and unprofessional, but I tried to remember that it was "show biz" and not the real world. *Pull yourself together, Annie,* I said to myself, once again quoting Dad. His words echoed in my mind as I drove down Russell Avenue with its stately, tall skinny palm trees. Orson Welles was a genius, but reputed to be an arrogant ogre. I knew I wouldn't stand a chance. I knew nothing about movies! But I was determined to give it a go.

So what I needed now was a crash course on Orson Welles: the man, his life, and his movies. And I didn't have much time.

I took off my "interview garb," slipped into a black sweat suit—no time for a swim that day. I drove to Samuel French's bookstore on the Strip for more information. The famous Sunset Boulevard starts in downtown Los Angeles, winds twenty-five miles through the Sunset Strip past fancy boutiques and gourmet restaurants, UCLA, Pacific Palisades, and ends at the beach.

I navigated the Strip amidst limousines and fancy cars, passing elegant window displays, famous nightclubs such as the Whisky a Go-Go, Comedy Store and the Roxy, outdoor cafes often frequented by celebrities, usually discovered by clusters of photographers. Perched in the hills above the Strip is the legendary castle-like hotel, the Chateau Marmont Hotel, Restaurant and Bar, which attracts a rock 'n' roll and movie crowd. It is well-known for its exclusivity and privacy. Original landmarks of luxury and style, the Beverly Hills Hotel and the Hotel Bel Air entice a wealthy celebrity clientele. There are "power" restaurants where agents, actors and others in show business go to be seen or to make deals. *L.A. Story*, a favorite film of mine with Steve Martin, has a delightful scene at a fancy restaurant, a table of about a dozen "Hollywood types" ordering coffees, each one described in minute detail, which the patient waiter somehow records.

My red baseball cap protected me from the hot sun, but not from my racing thoughts. I wasn't on the ladder desperately climbing to success in Hollywood, but what I did want was an emotional and intellectual jolt into vitality. The worst that could happen was that I'd make a fool of myself.

In the bookstore, the sections on writing, acting, and directing were particularly busy, with hungry hopefuls groping for titles that might offer them knowledge or guidance on how to enter and take the necessary steps to succeed in their craft. I was overwhelmed by the number of books on Orson Welles in about fifteen of the twenty or more sections. I spent the next two hours delving into Orson's life, which was comprehensively described in so many of the books I took off the shelves.

Citizen Kane set a precedent for Orson's future film career: critical raves, but unsuccessful at the box office. He moved to Europe for thirty years, where financial backing was more forthcoming than in Hollywood. His reputation preceded him as a high-risk genius, always trying to raise money but consistently running over budget. I wondered how Orson's self-imposed exile affected him personally. How did he survive his lifelong battle as an artist battling investors? His films were sometimes taken over and completed by others, often unbeknownst to him while he was in Europe.

Tragic.

Whatever the outcome of my interview tomorrow, I was astounded by the prolific amount of information on this man, and wanted to see all of his films and read everything written about him.

Leaving the bookstore, I was struck with another problem. Did I want to look professional for my interview? Sexy? Business-like? Whatever I wore, I wanted to feel as snappy as possible. At home, my cats, Magic Kelly and Charlie Dickens circled my ankles in adoration and hunger, purring and meowing me into the kitchen. They looked alike with long black fur, sleek builds, unrelated orphan kittens I had saved.

Poring over outfits, fresh from soaking in a lavender-scented bath, I decided to wear my recently purchased black suit, together with a crisp white shirt which appeared professional, but feminine. I left the shirt open at the top to soften the look and allowed for a simple marquisite pendant to rest on my cleavage. Black tights, flat shoes.

Chapter 18

MEETING ORSON

The next morning, I drove along Santa Monica Boulevard into the gridlock of Beverley Hills, my little old car surrounded by sleek, long, luxurious vehicles. I passed by Spanish mansions with thick clusters of birds of paradise, Hawaiian ginger, banana palms and other tropical plants bordering lush, green lawns. Fleeting rainbows caught my eye from the sprinklers which sprayed back and forth. An enchanting sight for a limey chick.

It was March, 1974. Hot and dry. I loved the weather though I missed the rain at times. The rain in England fell almost daily, allowing the glory of endless fields of velvet green, but the wet gloomy days depressed my spirits. My stomach churned as I drove through the neighborhoods of small apartment buildings and detached houses bordering Century City, an empire of concrete, glass and steel high-rises.

This was a business center housing powerful law and accounting firms, many connected with film, television and music. They seemed cold, gray and impersonal. My jitters caused me to miss the hotel, requiring a detour of several blocks to arrive where I was supposed to be. The semi-circular driveway was littered with stretch limos, ostentatious cars and elegantly uniformed bellhops.

I parked in front of one of those annoying "Valet Parking Only" signs, incurring expense and wasted time when I was ready to leave the building. A young man in a navy and red uniform gave me a ticket as he opened my door. "Have a nice day!" he said cheerfully, flooring my accelerator and disappearing into a tunnel with my car. I squinted upward. The buildings seemed to disappear into the sky, stark and gray. The balconies were permanently lit. The Century Plaza Hotel boasted an opulent lobby adorned with huge vases of exotic flower arrangements and tall, elegant palms, artistically placed. Curvaceous architecture. Rich, velvet couches and chairs in shades of peach and sage. Dark woods. Beveled glass. Art deco lamps were on mahogany tables. I was directed to the elevator in the "Reagan Tower," as it was then called. The penthouse was on the twentieth floor. I started taking deep breaths.

In the elevator, a stooped lady in a camel hair coat gave me a gracious nod and limped out at the eleventh floor. I boldly pushed the "twenty" button. There was no turning back. When the doors slid open, a gold-leaf sign pointed right.

"Penthouse." There was no bell on the elegantly carved, pearl white double doors. I forced myself to knock firmly. A voice bellowed from within, "It's open!"

The sun momentarily blinded me as I entered the huge suite, which was surrounded by three walls of windows. As my sight adjusted to the intense brightness, I saw him. At the far end of the room sat a massive figure surrounded by purple in a sturdy wooden armchair. A pleasant odor of cigar smoke wafted toward me. Suppressing my jitters, I marched right up to him and thrust out my hand.

"I am honored to meet you, Mr. Welles. I'm..."

His mellifluous voice boomed at me.

"Call me Orson. Everyone calls me Orson."

He seemed warm and friendly, not what I had been expecting. A royal purple terrycloth bathrobe surrounded his rotund frame. His swollen feet and ankles in tight grey stockings rested on a footstool. Brown-framed glasses sat half-way down on his nose. He scrutinized me with dark, intense eyes which seemed to x-ray through me, as though he could have read into my very being. He broke my intimidation by gesturing me to a chair opposite him. I handed him my two-page resume, neatly fastened into a red folder. He tossed it onto the table between us amidst books, legal pads, pens in a hotel mug, piles of paper, two telephones, a fax machine, an elegant cigar box and an ashtray.

"Andre said you wanted to work for me. I need a personal and film production assistant... to be by my side and do a bit of everything for me. I am sure you have heard lots of gossip about me. Maybe some of it is true, maybe some is not. What should I know about you?" he inquired, staring at me intensely.

I was unprepared for the scope and the weight of his question. My answer would determine my fate. In the middle of my restlessness the previous night, it dawned on me that Orson's entire life was about stories. He was an entertainer. He must have hated to be boring. I had to inspire him, leave him with a memory of me that was impressive. My brain had chattered on until I had finally fallen asleep.

Then miraculously, as though summoned, a sunbeam settled like a butterfly on a large cobalt blue glass ashtray.

"I could describe my skills, responsibilities, the variety and descriptions of jobs I have worked in London and here in L.A. But Orson, I would prefer to be more personal than that." I astonished myself, launching into the role I had envisioned in the bath last night. My tone sounded commanding! Maybe, just maybe, he was slightly intrigued. I took another deep breath.

"When I was about the age of ten, living in a small, gossipy town in northern England, I started thinking about my life. I was surrounded by complacency. Nobody seemed to have dreams for themselves, except to stay in the old country, get married, have kids, and frequent the pubs. I was mystified. Surely there had to be more to life."

I leaned forward, elbows on my knees, hoping to be more engaging. "One day I was in my parents' bedroom and I noticed, under the glass of my mother's dressing table, at the back, a postcard with palm trees on it, yellowed with age. I realized she must have had a dream once and told no one. In that moment, that became *my* dream. California."

Orson seemed to listen with some interest. But I sensed that I must add some punch to my voice.

"From that moment on, I wanted to flee to California, to follow the sun and find myself as a person. I was finally on a Pan Am flight to L.A. with a green card in my hand! In the aircraft, I was surrounded by leathery Texans in pointed leather cowboy boots, wearing gaudy turquoise jewelry. They saw how frightened I was. I knew no one in L.A., had no work, and had borrowed money to get here."

Orson's eyes became distant; his interest was slipping away. I quickened my pace and spoke more dramatically, plowing through my tale. I refused to be intimidated by Orson.

"The Texans kept feeding me whiskey shots which sedated my nerves. Smashed, flying over the sprawl of Los Angeles, I asked one of the drunken Texans, 'What are all those blue dots down there?'"

"'Why, little lady, them there are *swimmin' pools!*' They all guffawed."

Orson chuckled with amusement, or did he think I was a fool?

"Questions for me, Orson?"

Orson locked his eyes with mine, and with a hint of a smile declared, "You are spunky! Can you start now?" I was flabbergasted. I wanted to leap in the air, arms flailing about, shrieking and yelling out, "I got the job! I work for Orson Welles, the cinematic genius!"

I decided to retain my seemingly calm demeanor, merely exclaiming, "Thank you!"

"We will work here until we move into offices at the Samuel Goldwyn Studios. And then we will go on location, probably to Arizona."

He chose an enormous cigar from the box, lighting it with one of his long matches, and rested it on that divine ashtray. He grabbed the receiver off one of the telephones.

"Give me Housekeeping," he barked. His abrupt change of tone startled me. Not wanting to appear as though I were eavesdropping, I wandered around the suite in a daze exclaiming to myself, *I cannot believe it. I got the job!*

I curbed my excitement and went to check out the area assigned to me. There was a work desk for me, a refrigerator, Georgian-style couches and chairs in the sitting areas, a luxury bathroom in mirrors and marble with black and yellow towels stacked around the Jacuzzi bath. A huge bedroom held a variety of silk and velvet pillows on the bed, and clothes strewn about. It felt too personal to be peeking into his bedroom so I quickly retreated to the living area.

"My dry cleaning should have been delivered three hours ago. Where it is?" Orson barked into the phone. His words were alarmingly ferocious.

I wondered how the person at the other end of the phone was feeling; daunted, at least. I thought, optimistically, that the dry cleaning mess had allowed me to experience Orson's anger, and I now understood his absolute intolerance for inefficiency or mistakes. I must be forceful and assertive. I must not be crushed by Orson's gargantuan power, else it would lead to the end of my job, not to mention a vital part of me, my ego, my sense of self.

"I want it sent up NOW!" His voice thundered through the suite.

I escaped onto one of the balconies to separate myself from the power of his phone call.

As I scanned the view, hot air blew into my face. The swimming pool lay twenty floors below, surrounded by royal blue umbrellas and chaise lounges. My eyes swept across the L.A. skyline, the mountains in the distance, the Griffith Park Observatory and the Hollywood sign nestled into the hills. I was in the clouds. I worked for Orson Welles! Well today, that was. There I went again, tempering myself with negativity. After a moment, I cautiously stepped back into the room.

"I dislike inefficiency," he proclaimed. "It's an unfortunate characteristic that seems to run rampant in society today. Enough of that," he said, handing me a yellow pad and a pen. We sat across from one another at his table. I couldn't control the trembling in my hands. He puffed on his cigar, thinking intensely.

"Call Gary."

I looked at him in puzzlement.

"Gary Graver. He's my cinematographer." His tone was sarcastic. I felt ignorant and dared not utter a word. I simply jotted down everything he said and decided to deal with it later.

"Set up a meeting here for whatever his schedule allows, to discuss lenses, filters, film stock, etc. Then," he rattled on. I wrote furiously. "...find John Huston — he's probably roaming about in Europe or Mexico. Tell him to contact me as soon as possible. It's about the role, Jake Hannaford. Tell Patrick at Ma Maison I'll be an hour late for lunch. There will be three of us today. The number's unlisted—you will need this."

He handed me a frayed, thick, black address book. "If you lose this book, my world will end." I shuddered at his threatening words as I continued to scribble frantically.

"Find out about house rentals in the Scottsdale area for about 3-4 months — spacious, at least five bedrooms, a pool — call Henry. Henry. That's J-a-g-l-o-m. Ask if he is free for lunch tomorrow at one at the saloon."

My feelings of inadequacy flooded me. Was his pace quickening or was it my panic?

"I want to meet with Susan Strasberg. Is she in town? Is she working? Find out from her agent."

A knock at the door rescued me from his incessant string of demands. I opened the door and several pieces of clothing on wooden hangers were handed to me by a faceless arm.

"Thank you," I said, as I heard Orson mutter under his breath, "About time." He got up from the chair, tightening the belt to his robe. "Hang them in the bathroom and remove all that plastic waste. And call Birns & Sawyer. Talk to John there. I will need a pee-wee and a western, ten seniors and two juniors. And two broads and three babies."

What on earth was he talking about? Broads and babies? Dare I ask him for clarification?

"Also, I'll need an Inky and an Obie. Ask him about availability towards the end of April. I want them on hold, but I don't know the duration of our shoot yet."

I did not know it then, of course, but if the Internet had been available at that time, Google would have saved me! My mouth fell open as Orson closed the bathroom door behind him. I was in a confused fog.

How would I do this? Would every hour of every day be demanding like this? I screamed inside. My father's voice stepped in: *Slow down and be practical, Annie.* His words helped me to focus on my notes. I tried to decipher my scribbles. First, I had to call about his lunch. I checked through the M's in his black book for the telephone number. I picked up the receiver and asked the operator: "How do I get an outside line?" I tracked down Patrick at the restaurant, giving him Orson's message about lunch.

"Who are you?" he asked.

"I'm Annie, Orson's new assistant," I gulped, owning my new title.

"Hope to meet you soon, Annie," he said warmly.

"Me too! Where is the Saloon, Patrick?"

"Here!" He laughed.

I hung up just as Orson reappeared, white hair slicked back, cigar between his fingers, black jacket, grey trousers, white shirt buttoned at the neck with the same grey stockings, dark grey slippers.

"By the way, I want to meet with Bogdanovich A.S.A.P."

"Patrick has your message about lunch," I said firmly.

He nodded in response, choosing one of several canes propped up by the door. He turned back to me and gestured to his work table.

"You will find the Studio and Academy Player Directories helpful. Locate one if you can. And make sure you get yourself some lunch, Annie."

He closed the door behind him. The suite was suddenly peaceful, devoid of Orson's majestic physical and emotional presence. I delighted in the silence and started to breathe more normally. He had called me by my name!

I hoped his lunch would be long. I wanted to accomplish at least some of his demands while I was alone. My stomach grumbled, but I didn't have the luxury of time to stop for food. I moved a telephone, the telephone directory, the address book, pads and pens over to my work table. I angled it to avoid the direct sunlight and to improve my city view.

I found some of the names and telephone numbers in Orson's tattered address book, which I handled delicately. John Huston had about nine different numbers. I plowed through the three-inch thick address book finding endless lists of leading actors and actresses, ingénues, character actors, agents and business managers. I put in a desperate call to my party host from the other night, Scotty. I quickly filled him in on what had transpired.

"WOW! Congratulations," he said. "I..."

I interrupted him in panic, asking him about the babies, broads, and juniors, apparently an assortment of lights for film-making. He gave me the number for Birns & Sawyer, a studio equipment rental house in Hollywood.

"Do you have the Studio Directory?" Scotty asked. "It lists artists and casting agents, production and costume companies, the guilds, and so on. You'll need it. I'll have my secretary messenger one over to you right now. The Century Plaza?"

"Yes," I answered in relief. "We are in the penthouse suite, twentieth floor."

He laughed wholeheartedly, exclaiming, "You big-wig, you!" He hung up after wishing me good luck. I was beyond grateful to him for his guidance. I made persistent calls to contact the people Orson wanted, but usually reached secretaries or answering services. However, I did manage to catch Gary Graver and arranged a meeting for five o'clock the following day. Gary was friendly and easy-going. "If you need any help at all, just ask me — I've been working with Orson for a long time — good luck, kid!"

Henry Jaglom would lunch with Orson at one o'clock tomorrow. I left messages with Bogdanovich's secretary and Susan's agent who was at lunch. With John Huston, I started with the asterisked number in Las Caletas. The girl who answered spoke no English and the extent of my Spanish was *buenas dias* and *cerveza*. I deduced that John was not there, but left her an urgent message to have him call. I phoned all the other numbers, a time-consuming task because of language difficulties, and left messages. Hopefully accurate ones.

The other phone rang. "Orson Welles' assistant," I answered earnestly. A loud knock. "Hold on, please."

Surely Orson wasn't back yet? I rushed to the door and was handed a brown envelope addressed to me. It must be the directory from Scotty, a man of his word. I sighed in relief.

"How can I help you?" I said as I picked up the phone again.

"It's Bob, Susan Strasberg's agent... is Orson there?"

"He will return in an hour or so. He wants to know if Susan is in town or if she is working."

"She's in Paris, returning in two weeks." I boldly asked for and received her telephone number, realizing that there was power in working for Orson. His name ignited flustered disbelief or silence, but either way I got the attention I needed. After clarifying with the operator that Scottsdale was in Arizona, I called the Chamber of Commerce. I described what we needed and wrote down a list of real estate/house rental companies, leaving my home phone number to call if anything became available in April.

The sound of a key in the door. Orson entered, greeted me with a nod, and disappeared into the bathroom. I continued my research, hoping that some of my accomplishments would be acceptable.

"Thank you, Annie," he said. "I need to tell you that I am an insomniac, and may take naps during the day." Maybe, hopefully now, because I had so much to do. No such luck. "What's the story?" he asked, lighting and puffing on another cigar.

I grabbed my pad and pen from my worktable and started explaining to him about meetings confirmed and messages left, where and with whom, and I informed him that I had given my home telephone number for the real estate rental people in Arizona, quickly saying, "I thought you'd receive less phone calls by my taking them at home. I hope that is all right with you. I have put my number under 'A' in your book in case you need it, or want to transfer calls over to me."

"Thank you." He appeared drowsy despite those intense eyes.

"Is there a copy machine in the hotel? I would like to copy my notes for you."

"Business center, 4th floor," he answered. "Why don't you go now? You can copy my address book so you will always have my important numbers." As an afterthought, "I am trusting you, you know."

"You can," I replied sincerely.

"You'll need this," he said, handing me the room key.

I was back in the elevator, reminding myself of the wretched agony of several hours ago. It seemed like weeks ago. So much had happened. I pressed the floor button, more confidently this time, cradling Orson's precious book in my hands. At the fourth floor, I found my way down a bare, wood-paneled hallway, its cool ambiance a sharp contrast to the welcoming elegance and color the rest of hotel.

I entered the business center, turned on the copy machine, implored it—do not jam! I usually had lousy luck with anything mechanical or electric, but please, not today. I started copying each page, some of which were frayed, with the utmost care. I was in awe at all the famous names listed. More importantly, I was in awe that Orson had entrusted me with his address book. We had met only hours ago. I felt chuffed that he must have some belief in me.

I slid the plastic key into the penthouse door. Orson still sat on the couch, wedged between cushions, stroking his beard, lost in thought. I hesitated, then seeing his eyes suddenly light, handed him his address book and a copy of our day's notes, listing what was complete and incomplete, contact names and telephone numbers.

I showed him the copy of his address book, assuring him that no eyes would see it except for ours. As a mischievous promise, I said, "No magician will have power over it!"

"Clever, aren't you?" he chuckled. "John Huston called me back to say he will play the role of Jack Hannaford and will travel to Arizona as soon as we have a production timeline. After all these years, he still pressures me for a script!" He laughed, incredulously. "He knows there will be no script for him; he is more spontaneous and real with speech outlines, like many actors."

"No script?" I asked.

"The ideas are all that matter. Memorized lines sound stilted. A film must be alive, real, not stifled by limitations. Taking risks gives vitality to filmmaking and to life in general. You'll see that when we start shooting."

"I think I know what you mean. My spirit started to die in England when smothered by so many limitations."

"That's right. Don't forget to call me when you arrive home."

I can still hear his words: "When we start shooting!"

Already, Orson believed in me enough to think about our work together in Arizona. I had survived a positive and productive day!

Chapter 19

WHIRLWIND

The valet roared up in my old MG, counted out my dollar bills to ensure the wad covered the parking charge and his tip, and I was on the road again. Bach's *Magnificat* reflected my triumphant mood as I drove through the concrete jungle of Century City towards Hollywood. I screeched back into my carport, with squealing brakes to punctuate my day of success. Gathering up my work, I ran up the stairs, oblivious to the swimming pool, which was usually my salvation at day's end.

Magic and Dickens welcomed me with their ritualistic dance around my ankles, purring constantly, ready for affection and food.

I called Orson to check in and exchange information. He gave me updates for his calendar. I asked him for his FAX number so that the real estate agents could send over any photographs and details of houses to rent in Arizona. Orson suggested I return to his office at eight in the morning, before his meeting with Bogdanovich.

"Call me if you need anything," I said.

An unwise offer. My telephone rang in the middle of the night. I struggled in the dark to pick up the receiver, frightened that my father had suffered another debilitating attack of bronchitis. Orson's commanding voice relieved that fear, but after waking me up, he ordered, "Locate Mercedes McCambridge!"

I squinted at my bedside clock. "It's three in the morning! Tomorrow, Orson. I will find Mercedes for you tomorrow." I hung up and snuggled under the covers again. Guilt and self-doubt surged through me. How dare I say "no" on the first day of my job? I could be fired now. Was I nuts? I was a peon, and he was a world-famous genius. I started to dial him back, but my fingers froze as a thought entered my mind: *I must assert boundaries for myself, and for him, too.* Otherwise, I would be on call constantly, eventually becoming a physical and emotional wreck. To function, I needed at least six of hours of sleep per night. So I decided not to call Orson back. How I behaved now would set a precedent for our future working relationship. I must learn to respect myself. I also wanted Orson to respect me.

Each day I learned to cope with Orson's complex personality and his endless demands, constantly learning about the process of filmmaking. I questioned others, most of whom were in filmmaking themselves, and after several days of "proving myself," I became daring enough to ask Orson himself about some of his orders, which to my relief, he answered patiently.

I spent many hours each day as a detective, tracking down famous personalities such as Lilli Palmer, Susan Strasberg, Norman Foster, Dennis Hopper, Rich Little, Claude Chabrol, Paul Mazursky, Frank Marshall, and many more. I was persistent and diplomatic. I started to learn the art of being assertive, never accepting "no" as a response.

When we moved into the Goldwyn office suite, I quickly realized that my attention must remain focused on Orson, informing those new on board that I was his personal and film assistant, not Girl Friday to everyone. I felt slightly more at ease now that I was working around cast and crew who could offer their knowledge and support to me.

I collapsed into bed each night trying to relax from the intensity of the day, however the struggle between exhaustion and adrenaline took at least one hour each night to abate.

I was on three telephone lines at the same time when Orson walked in, accompanied by a stunning beauty. He introduced her as his collaborator and partner, Oja Kodar. Her long black hair was pulled back to accentuate delicate, high cheekbones, dark, piercing eyes, and a delicate olive complexion. Her English was impeccable, though she spoke with a slight Hungarian accent.

She had trained as a physicist and mathematician, but now was renowned as a successful sculptor, artist, actress, writer, producer and director. I was told she was a gifted chess player, too. Initially, I felt intimidated by Oja's beauty and her multiple talents, but as time passed, I turned my fear around to start thinking of her as a role model for myself.

I finally learned about the movie, the title of which was *The Other Side of the Wind*. It had been started by Orson, Oja Kodar and Gary Graver in 1970. Orson funded the production outside of the Hollywood system, actors and crew being proud to work for him for minimal pay. Sadly, the film had been plagued by legal battles, feuds, and difficulties with raising funds.

Oja, Orson, and Kiki, his little black Scottie, and I moved into a big house rented in Carefree, Arizona, several miles from Scottsdale. My pets were being lovingly watched by a neighbor friend, also an avid animal lover.

I wondered how the three of us would get along under one roof. Oja was opinionated, sharing mutual respect with Orson. I needed to view her as "part" of Orson. I quickly learned that as long as I could claim a few moments to be completely alone to check in with myself, often in the privacy of a bathroom, I could preserve my physical and emotional strength, keeping our relationships harmonious.

I knew that I was exhausted, having been swept along at an intense pace since the first day with Orson. I certainly gained the "jolt" I had yearned for. The movie had become my entire life, with no time or energy for anything else. The cast and crew were my new "family." When I informed my British family and L.A. friends about my new position, the reaction had been surprisingly mixed — from envy and admiration to, "What about a real job?"

The house in Arizona was a hubbub of creativity, warmth, and inspiration, the atmosphere sparkling. It was surrounded by desert, huge boulder formations and hundreds of varieties of cacti, my favorite being the stately saguaro, its phallic columns always dramatic against the clear Arizona sky.

I was thrilled to meet John Huston, a striking presence, stylishly dressed in greys. Slim, with a white beard, handsome in that craggy way, and all topped off with a black fedora. Orson, almost always in his purple robe, greeted him exuberantly with open arms, heartfelt affection, and laughter.

They initially spent several hours by the pool, smoking cigars, exchanging colorful tales of Ireland, both of them having lived there, and discussing the film. I remember having a stimulating conversation with Huston myself about Africa, a place that had always fascinated me, where he'd shot *The African Queen*.

Later, when John tried to memorize some of his lines, Orson said impatiently, "John, don't act the words, just say what you want! What's important to you, the actor, is what happened yesterday — and what happened twenty years ago. The ideas are all that matter."

Chapter 20

THE SHOOT

After the first day of shooting in Arizona, I realized that Orson took the needed controls to position the camera, lights, describe how the sound should be mixed, and work with all the actors and actresses to create vital dialogue and relationships. Sometimes a shot was completed in one take, sometimes it took more than twenty or thirty takes. But whenever Orson exclaimed, "Oh-kay! CUT!" a powerful silence permeated the set, everyone knowing that magic had been born.

I pinched myself to let myself know that these days and nights were the most real and exhilarating of any I had ever experienced in my life. Yet this was filmmaking, the ultimate illusion!

When we had first set up in Carefree, Orson asked me to buy two dozen or more brandy snifters, more set props, I assumed. But at the end of the first day's shoot, Orson asked for the snifters, pouring out generous amounts of Courvoisier for each of us.

"Time to celebrate the day!" Orson exclaimed. We all gathered around as he held court each night, cigar and brandy in hand, spinning yarns about his life and filmmaking, and tossing out philosophical ideas and questions for discussion. He captivated us with his brilliance, humor, and charm. He performed coin and card magic tricks, flooring us with his talent. A true magician. I had never known this level of camaraderie and teamwork, all of us exhilarated and inspired by our involvement in *The Other Side of the Wind*.

But it was morning all too soon. I'd drag myself out of bed, threw on jeans and a t-shirt, and helped set up for our 7 a.m. call. Day after day.

One night at three o'clock in the morning a few weeks into the shoot, I was awakened by urgent pounding at my door. Convinced that something terrible had occurred, I leapt out of bed, still disoriented, and pulled open the door.

Orson stood there, wild-eyed. "I want you to call our investor in Paris."

"I will call as soon as I get up. I need my sleep!" I quickly shut the door, relieved that once again I had not complied and that I had set my boundaries.

But I could feel that something *was* wrong. Usually, when I arrived on the set bright and early, Orson, Oja, and Gary were already busy scrutinizing the schedule and generally bustling about, but on this morning they were behind closed doors, loud voices resounding from within.

When Gary finally appeared, he tensely pointed at several of us to go outside with him. My stomach filled with dread. I breathed deeply, the air refreshingly cool, no sunlight dancing on the swimming pool yet.

"I have bad news," Gary announced gravely. "We are almost out of funds, and will have to shut down production within a week, maybe sooner. I'm really sorry to say this but it's a wrap for all of you, as of now."

Gary's words floated through a wind tunnel. My world crashed. I was paralyzed. I felt peculiar, lightheaded. Was I going to faint? His next words shocked me into reality. "Apparently our funds have been embezzled. We have no idea what happened. Orson will call you back as soon as we have funds again."

Responding to our grim expressions, he said, "I'm devastated, too."

On a Southwest flight back to L.A., I was wedged in the middle seat between two spiffy salesmen blabbing on about their company's products. Irritated by their exuberant dollar talk, I asked if they'd mind if I switched to the aisle seat, which I did, and I was finally able to settle back and close my eyes.

The lines between nightmares and reality collided in my head. I had been ruthlessly severed from Orson, the film, and about eighty other movie folks, famous and otherwise, and from myself and my new identity as a movie industry professional. What was to become of me now? No Orson, no family, no home. Now what? How would I cope with my "normal" life? What *was* my normal life? I ordered a double Bloody Mary from the petite, cheery stewardess (they weren't called "flight attendants" then) and slugged each mini bottle down over ice. I ignored my seat companion's comments about my quick consumption, and managed to calm down a bit for the duration of the flight.

I missed my family of friends, Orson, the Arizona air, the light, and being an intimate part of our creative project; I was lost. Once back home in Hollywood, I flopped onto the couch. My apartment felt cramped and silent. My cats could not be coaxed out of their usual hiding places, even after using their favorite toys with bells and feathers on a long, dangly pole. After a few hours, Magic and Dickens finally shed their nonchalant airs, forgave my absence, and followed me from room to room, nuzzling me for attention. Their greetings offered me some comfort.

I gave myself a week of physical and emotional recuperation. I stayed home with my cats, soaked in bubble baths, listened to the comforting strains of Chopin, Brahms, and Mozart, and constantly reflected on my film experience.

I cried my way through *Citizen Kane* and inched my way through two books on Orson, continuing to yearn for our movie life in Carefree.

I phoned Robert, who had been, I felt, indirectly responsible for getting me into all this by inviting me to that party, expecting to hear his chirpy recording, but he picked up! Between my sobs, he listened, ordering me to meet him for dinner later. I managed to sink into a doze, reassured that all of Scotty's years of working on films would help me cope with the loss I had just suffered.

Four paws gently wandered around my body, back and forth. Whiskers tickled my face...

"Dickens!" I squinted, now fully awake. Magic was sprawled on a velvet throw over the top of the couch, staring down at both of us. Eyes intense. I sat up to be comforted by purrs, licks, nuzzles, and nudges, a loving welcome home for them, and for me.

The cats jumped off the couch, circled my ankles, and then led me into the kitchen where I opened a can of their favorite food and ladled it into their bowls. They scarfed off the whole lot. They waited for more, stared at me with pleading eyes, until I told them, "That's enough for right now."

Later, I drove down the narrow, winding streets to my favorite restaurant, Musso and Frank's Grill on Hollywood Boulevard, a "glamorous" landmark since 1919 with elderly waiters "as crusty as the bread," newly-designed printed menus daily, and justifiably famous martinis. Sidewalks swarmed with tourists posing with costumed characters such as Batman in front of Grauman's Chinese Theater. Open-top tour buses were en route to see movie studios, stars' homes, the elegant boutiques on Rodeo Drive, the landmark Farmer's Market, and other world-famous sites.

Scotty was waiting in one of the red leather booths, and greeted me with a sympathetic hug, during which I burst into uncontrollable sobs. He handed me a wad of tissues.

"My work wasn't good enough!" I lamented.

"It's not about you. Lay-offs and shut-downs are a major part of the business. And sadly, Orson is famous for overspending and running out of funds."

A long-nosed, solemn waiter loomed above our table, order pad poised, and waited indifferently for my emotional outburst to be concluded. Scotty quickly ordered martinis, straight up, Kettle One vodka, olives, and two orders of sand dabs with extra lemon.

"Now go away, Sunshine," Scotty muttered under his breath and I managed a giggle through the sodden tissues.

"I never said goodbye, not even to Orson!" I wailed on, tears pouring down my cheeks again. Scotty listened and thankfully didn't try to appease me, knowing I had to cope with the painful end to a thrilling experience in my own way. "At least in the film business the unpredictable is predictable," he said. "You have to be ready for anything to happen."

"Worst of all is the sudden loss of a huge family. It's tearing me apart."

He shrugged. "Give yourself a break; you've only just arrived home. You had probably reached that stage where a large number of cast and crew have figured out how to blend personalities, cope with the director, producer, and the actor's demands, an endless web of psychological intrigue. The director is the psychiatrist to everyone. And then in a flash, the production dies. A lack of funds, over budget, critical businessmen who know zilch about film."

In the parking lot, I thanked him profusely for his listening and support. He told me to be extra careful about driving after the martinis. I assured him that I would drive slowly and safely home, where I would hide under the covers for the rest of my life.

Chapter 21

OUT OF WORK IN HOLLYWOOD

I shall never put myself through an experience like that again," I said with finality to anyone who would listen. "No more show biz for me. That's it. I need a stable job again offering security, sick pay, bonuses, and a pension plan — a regular nine-to-five."

I had suddenly become the poster child for the classic Hollywood dilemma: on top of the world when working, miserable (and broke) when not working.

Being out of work in Hollywood is the pits. Clearly, I would need to start looking for a new job. But after working with Orson, how dull would that be? From the magic of films, to what – waitressing at Denny's? *Get a grip, Annie,* I kept telling myself. *Remember where you came from. You fled all that gloom and eternal rain. You may be out of work, but just look at that glorious sun!*

One Sunday while scrutinizing the *L.A. Times,* I was caught by a large ad that read, "We seek a pharmaceutical representative with a bachelor's degree and past medical experience for sales in the Hollywood territory. The company, based in New York, offers a great salary, commission, a company car, and an expense account." Well, I thought, I had finally gotten my bachelor's degree, so I should probably use it for something.

Despite my total lack of interest in the pharmaceutical industry, I put together a resume, typed a cover letter, and handed the envelope to the cheery mailman as he finished depositing letters into each of the apartment building's twelve mailboxes.

Two days later, Don Russell, the District Manager of VSU Pharmaceutical Company, phoned me to come in for an interview.

Following directions, I drove west on the Ventura Freeway to the Vagabond Inn in Woodland Hills. I was half-hearted about the position, and then especially troubled when I learned that the interview would be held in a hotel room, which seemed highly inappropriate for a professional position. I was directed to a creaky, padded elevator reminding me of a jail cell. I held my breath, the elevator's shuddering grind triggering my worst nightmare of entrapment. To my relief, it quaked to a halt and finally the squeaky doors opened on the fourth floor, where Don greeted me with a cheerful grin and a firm, warm handshake.

He was short and had wavy hair, was very jolly, and dressed in a short-sleeved tan shirt, a beige tie, and brown trousers. A symphony of dullness.

He read through my resume, suddenly stopping in astonishment.

"*Citizen Kane* is my favorite film! Orson Welles is brilliant! How did you like working for him?"

I was drawn to his curiosity and ebullience.

"I did," I said.

"I've heard he can be an ogre," Don went on.

"Not to me," I replied proudly. "But I had to learn to stand up for myself. He's very demanding, but brilliant, vital, and loves to laugh. He taught me about filmmaking and, unbeknownst to him, many lessons about life." My mind flooded with visions of dear Orson.

"I've been a real movie buff since I was a kid. Why on earth are you here? Why don't you seek work in film? You have one helluva reference."

"Frankly, I need a secure job with all of the perks that you offer. Filmmaking is so unpredictable; shut-downs and layoffs are a big part of the business."

After an easy hour of interview, Dan exclaimed, "Slam dunk! You're hired!" He gave me a business card and another vigorous handshake, grinning with boyish charm and sincerity. "Besides, I like the accent. It will impress clients."

I accepted the job with its many perks, which is what I wanted. I was sent for a two-week intense training at the company headquarters in Tuckahoe, New York, in an elegant grey stone mansion amidst manicured lawns and rose bushes. By the time I returned to Los Angeles, my apartment was already stacked high with a large delivery of boxes. I unpacked the mess of product samples, literature and printed forms and piled them in my already crowded bedroom. Not only were Magic and Dickens giddy to have their mom home again, now there were mounds of new toys for them to sniff and play with.

The job allowed me the autonomy to visit doctor's offices, pharmacies, and hospitals whenever it suited me. I had the promised company car — a maroon-colored Chevy — and I parked my old beat-up MG on the street. I had an expense account and potential commissions added to the base salary which would give me that sense of security and professionalism that I had never felt before.

Much to my own surprise, I did very well as a pharmaceuticals detail salesperson, which taught me an important lesson: being good at something can sometimes be a *curse* if the thing you are good at doesn't interest you! But I hung in there.

Increasing the sales figures in my territory's pharmacies was the goal. Doctors and pharmacists were intrigued to meet a female representative, especially a British one, greeting me kindly and with curiosity. I sometimes presented formal product pitches, answering in-depth questions about the advantages of our company's drugs versus others. Building relationships and being honest and direct added to my sales figures. For more attention, I exaggerated my British accent while conducting myself professionally. I even became cheeky enough to ask directly, "Come on, Doc, write me some 'scripts,' would you?"

My record sales figures enabled me to work half-days only, my secret. After four pharmacy and three doctor visits, I went home, made a shrimp and avocado salad, and poured a cold Mackeson stout into an iced pub mug. I took a slug as I sank onto the couch and toasted the "autonomy and the freedom of success."

The most gratifying perk of steady employment was being able to send my sister, and then my parents, tickets to come to visit me in California. Prior to my parents' arrival, I bustled through last-minute preparations, stocking the fridge, buying foods and drinks that I knew they would enjoy. The downtown Los Angeles flower mart on a Saturday morning, open to the public, expands to the size of a football field, an exotic feast for the senses, with aisles and aisles of stalls, displaying gorgeous colors and fragrances, plants and flowers that take your breath away. I finally tore myself away to drive home, car laden with masses of blooms. I tastefully arranged the flowers in an assortment of glass and pottery vases, lovingly placed, making sure to put several in the guest bedroom and bathroom. Each room was now spotless, warm and welcoming, even the kitchen, the 'fridge filled with fresh California fruits and vegetables, herbs, supplies of lamb chops and chicken in the freezer. And on the dining table, a Chinese bowl filled with grapefruits, bananas, a pineapple, limes and lemons.

At the airport, my parents emerged from Customs and Immigration with big smiles and open arms, appearing vital despite the long journey from Devon to Heathrow Airport in London, then to California. A year had passed since my last visit home, but to my relief, Mum and Dad hadn't changed a bit.

My father beamed in contentment, basking in the hot sun for several days to overcome jet lag and "warm up." I didn't allow my Mum to lift a finger.

"Don't move from that lounge chair, Mum! It's about time you were spoiled rotten!" I said, serving her a cup of tea and an assortment of English biscuits.

My parents were not used to being told what to do or not do. But after a day or two, they relaxed and settled into their daughter's plans. We drove up Angeles Crest Highway into the local mountains to stay in a cabin amidst the forest of fir trees. "Like the woods surrounding a mini-Alpine village," exclaimed my mother.

We returned to our base, then on to Joshua Tree Monument in the desert, the barren landscapes, bizarre figures of the Joshua trees startling my parents. Then we explored the local seaside towns, always the background of the Pacific Ocean waves. We dined in restaurants where my father gorged on platters of fresh oysters, not believing the reasonable prices and the surrounding beauty. Much to my delight, my parents loved L.A. and all that Southern California had to offer. Even their first visit to a supermarket was overwhelming to them.

"I cannot believe all these aisles of fresh fruit and vegetables. And the amazing variety of fish, seafood and meats," Mum exclaimed. "Everything is cheap here! This is even better than all your descriptions, Annie!"

Dad agreed, stocking up on California wines, Harvey's Bristol Crème sherry and crème de menthe, my kitchen now packed with bottles of liquor on top of the fridge and counters. My Dad was chuffed, shocked by the bargain prices. I cannot remember his ever being so relaxed, the sun seeming to cast a "happy" spell over him, and despite my mother's dislike of heat, she gradually eased into wearing less clothing. She was awed to see her hubby so relaxed.

"I haven't heard a coughing bout or a wheeze from you since we arrived, Tom. Your body likes this climate!"

"No doubt about it." He grinned.

After a trip with breathtaking views up the Pacific Coast Highway, exploring the majesty of Yosemite National Forest, Kings and Sequoia Canyons, we returned to Los Angeles to prepare for my parents' departure. We agreed that the six weeks together were the happiest in our lives. My father laughed more than I can ever remember. I never dreamt that this "very British" couple would be enchanted by California. But they were. My mother's secret dream had come true.

My parents liked California so much, in fact, that several months later I was able to bring Mum and Dad back to Los Angeles and secure them positions as apartment managers of a building. The position came with perks, such as free rent in a furnished apartment, the opportunity to meet Americans, a job in which my Dad could fulfill his need to fix things, and a temporary stay of as many months as they wanted. They made friends quickly; people were drawn to their British charm, humor and warmth. I was proud of them. They bought an inexpensive older Ford Falcon, becoming proficient at driving around Los Angeles.

Whenever I was a passenger with them, I had a sense of *déjà vu* from long ago: Jacquie and me as youngsters, freezing cold in the back seat, moving along at Dad's slow speed, driving on the right side of the road.

No longer was I that green girl.

To my delight, my sister, after her divorce, decided to move to California too, with her son, Sean, and for a while we were all together as a "family" again. Both Jacquie and I were devastated when our parents ultimately had to return home. I missed them, very deeply, like never before. Mum and Dad had seen me as an adult, successful in my life endeavors, yet still as fun and quirky as they remembered. They agreed that I had bloomed in Los Angeles, and they now understood my life-long need for a feeling of freedom.

At least I still had Jacquie and my nephew, Sean.

Had it not been for pharmaceuticals fattening up my bank account, even my savings, none of that would have been possible.

Chapter 22

SIREN'S SONG

It was 1975, and the now historic Men's Singles Championship Final at Wimbledon between Arthur Ashe and Jimmy Connors, both of whom were top seeded, was to be shown on TV in Los Angeles later that day. All week long I had been anticipating this match with excitement, purposely avoiding the radio or TV so I wouldn't hear the results ahead of time. My plan was to leave work early and rush home. My avocado and shrimp salad and Mackson's were all waiting for me.

On my cheap black and white television, Arthur Ashe played with grace and power, easily winning the first two sets. I perched on the edge of the cushion, my heart racing. The crowd was yelling at Jimmy, their favorite, to rouse him to play with his usual level of passion in the hopes that he would win the third set, which he did with a stunning ace. He punched the air with his fist and the crowd roared in approval.

Arthur Ashe appeared unfazed. I desperately wanted *him* to win! He would make Wimbledon history, becoming the first black man to achieve the title.

I ignored the ringing phone, finished off the beer, rushed to the fridge for another, and noticed that my furry rascals had scoffed off the shrimps, leaving wilting iceberg lettuce strips behind. So, I'd have to do without the shrimp.

"Ashe leads two sets to one," declared the umpire.

The phone rang again. *Shut up!* Why on earth didn't I put it on answer mode?

The crowd was on their feet, cheering wildly. Both players sat near the umpire's chair to towel off, change shirts, and unwrap new racquets.

"C'mon Ashe," I exclaimed to Charlie Dickens who was now glued to the screen, just as I was. I grabbed the phone, distracted. "I'll call you back! I'm watching the Wimbledon final!" I slammed the receiver down impatiently.

Riiiiing! The damn phone rang AGAIN!

"What?!!?" I answered, loudly impatient.

"This is Orson Welles."

"Orson Welles," I repeated, confused and distracted. ORSON??? My brain spun in circles. ORSON! Orson on MY phone!!! I was speechless. Could this be true? How thrilling! A year had passed since that wretched day when I had to leave Orson and his movie. I managed to stammer, "I am SO glad to hear you... ummmm... I apologize for hanging up... I'm rude."

"Your spontaneity and directness helped me through hard times —positive qualities; don't ever think otherwise, Annie!"

I blushed at his compliment.

He declared, "My film is funded at last, and I want you to work for me again."

"Orson, I'd love to!" A shocked pause, and then I muttered weakly, "But I have a steady job now, which is lifting me out of financial crisis. I've been able to put money aside, help my family —"

"There's always a way to climb out of crisis, especially if you are passionate about what you do. But you're right. Steady work will always reap its rewards. Please think about it. You were almost perfect working for me!" He chuckled. "I will call you about this time tomorrow."

He wanted me back! I was bowled over by his compliment, but what about my regular paycheck? And the commissions? And the car? And the expense account? It was a regular job, but there was none of the thrill of working on the film, the personalities, the daily unpredictability and challenges.

I tried to distract myself by turning up the sound on the telly, yelling for Ashe to win, but because of Orson's call, my excitement was suddenly diminished, even when Ashe *did* win.

I had suddenly been spiraled into an excruciating dilemma; it kept me awake all that night, vacillating between passionate about the idea of working for Orson again, but afraid his production would inevitably lead to another shut- down leading to more pain and grief. But because of my "day" job in pharmaceuticals, I was actually *saving* money for the first time. Not only had I been able to bring my family to LA, but I had the luxury of buying new clothes instead of combing through thrift and resale shop aisles. I could pay to have my hair cut and dyed, and even sank into the luxury of weekly manicures and pedicures. I didn't want to agonize about money anymore. I was sick of it. With omnipotent strength, I rejected Orson's offer.

And I cried.

Chapter 23

CASTAWAYS

Several months later, Don invited me for lunch at the landmark Castaways Restaurant, perched high in the Burbank hills, and nicknamed "The Jewel on the Hill." Was I about to be fired? Reprimanded? I ran downstairs for a long swim. When I dove into the pool and started my laps, my rattling mind quieted and my senses were vitalized by the effect of cool water on my skin, sunlight playing with shade on the surface. I treasured those moments of peace within myself.

The lobby of the Castaways displayed an enormous tropical arrangement of white orchids, slender stalks of red ginger and several species of waxy heliconias. In blue jeans and an open-neck polo shirt, Don was more casually dressed than I had ever seen him, which heightened my nervousness about lunch. We waited for our table outside at one of the wrought iron patio tables and ordered drinks, enjoying the panoramic view of the golf course, Burbank, and the haze beyond.

"I guess I'm still puzzled as to why you left that gorgeous country, England, in the first place," Don was saying. "Have you ever regretted leaving?"

"Never. I belong in California. California is where I can pursue more fulfilling goals than settling down to be a proper England wife and mother and plant flowers. I can make my dreams real here."

"What *are* your dreams, Annie?"

I burst out laughing. "That's what I'm still trying to figure out! I've always envied people who know their life's mission at three. That was never the case with me."

Don seemed preoccupied. He ordered two more drinks from the waiter without asking me. I wondered if he wanted me to get tipsy. I was nervous; maybe he was, too.

When our table was ready, we moved into the dining room and sat beneath a hanging garden of flowing ferns and trailing philodendrons. Over Dungeness crab salads, Don raised his glass of J. Lohr Chardonnay for a toast. "Here's to your continued success, Annie." We clinked and sipped. Now was the time to pause and let him say what he had to say, rather than cook up another topic to chat about.

Don declared, "Bob, the president of the company, as you well know, and I agree on this — we want to promote you to become a medical trainer, which will mean a substantial increase in your salary and a much higher rank within the company."

I felt initially validated, but then plummeted into confusion. I blurted out, "I don't want a career in the pharmaceutical industry, Don."

Dismissing my comment as though not even listening, Don continued. "Unfortunately, the position is in New York at the very same headquarters where you were trained. The offer is bittersweet to me because I would lose you."

I cried out in dismay, "But Don, I don't *want* to live in New York!"

Don appeared crestfallen, but he still carried on with his sales pitch. "The company will pay for your relocation expenses and part of your rent. You could live in Tuckahoe Village—you know how quaint it is."

I squeezed his arm affectionately. "Thank you so much. I'm flattered, but I cannot leave L.A. Come on, Don, you know how much I love it here."

"Please think it over after I've given you more particulars. Okay?"

"Okay," I said, knowing my answer would be fixed.

I leaned forward. "Don, I never told you this, but about two months ago Orson Welles called to tell me that his film was funded again. He asked me to work for him again."

"Awesome! What did you say?"

"His offer threw me into a wretched dilemma, so I told him about my job with you, that I needed a steady income and time to think. I really wanted to take the offer, but I knew that he would run out of funds, close down production again, and I'd be back in the unemployment line. His follow-up call the next day was even more painful because he actually displayed his bitter disappointment. I love working in films, and I confess that the whole time I've worked for you I've had a secret plan to leave the company one day in order to return to working in a creative environment because it brings me joy and meaning. So you see why I cannot accept the promotion."

"I've known that, Annie, probably from the first day I met you. However, you have broken all sales records, and think of it, you are the first successful VSU saleswoman. A role model to the few women now on board, probably *because* of you. The sky is the limit for you in this company. Please think over our offer."

"Thank you, Don."

I thought about his offer until I turned down my street, delighting in the red and green neon sign, "Russell Arms," with palm trees curled around it. I knew what my final answer would be. I would leave pharmaceuticals forever.

As I entered my apartment, Magic and Charlie Dickens greeted me with urgent meows of hunger. I fed them, changed into my sweats, and flopped onto my comfy couch with my journal. I lay back among the cushions, as the intensity of the day sent me into a sweet oblivion.

Facing the reality of what I'd just done would have to wait until tomorrow.

Chapter 24

THE NAME THAT OPENS DOORS
IN HOLLYWOOD

"Have you gone off your rocker? Hollywood has jellied your brain!" a work colleague of mine at my pharmaceuticals job exclaimed when I told her I had turned down Don's promotion and had given notice in order to go back into the movie business.

Perhaps she was right. I'd gone loopy or why else would I be considering letting myself get pulled back into working in an industry where I knew that, sooner or later, there would be some kind of heart-break of the kind I had experienced before? But I just couldn't help it.

I began searching through the ads in the Hollywood trades, *The Reporter* and *Daily Variety* and what I discovered was that despite my time out for pharmaceuticals, Orson Welles was a name that opened doors in Hollywood.

My hefty several months of experience with Orson impressed British director Adrian Lyne enough to hire me as his assistant and coordinator of the team of designers and special effects people for Michael Douglas and his company on the pre-production of a film called *Starman*. I arranged to sit in on meetings with the Columbia Pictures executives, mostly men (not surprisingly at that time), often moody, erratic, and egocentric.

Adrian called everyone "luv," was down to earth, warm, witty, and very successful as the director of many slick, glossy commercials in the U.S. and throughout Europe. But creatively unsatisfied, he wanted to make films.

I missed Orson, his authenticity, blunt honesty, and his gargantuan personality. But I was back in filmmaking, amidst passionate, creative minds, vitality. I was "home."

Adrian's trailer, near the entrance of the studio, buzzed with activity; ideas flew around. Blueprints and models of the space alien and the spaceship covered the work tables.

When appropriate, I delighted in teasing Michael Douglas. I was a little "star struck" by his handsome demeanor and sexuality. I had a crush on him for years. Robert Redford passed by daily. He'd nod, tip his hat and say "hi" en route to his production office, which was near our trailer. I saw Clint Eastwood regularly, and like Redford, he was reserved, gentlemanly and affable. Having worked with many celebrities on Orson's picture, I had become at ease around the famous, but I was initially startled that this seemingly "ordinary" person was the "larger than life" celebrity seen on the big screen.

A collective spirit often starts to form from the beginning of any shoot, a group of individuals brought together to achieve the mutual goal of creating a film. A strong sense of camaraderie surfaces, the relationships usually light and harmonious, but when projects are shut down, the temporary friendships dissipate.

And that's what happened here. In spite of all the meetings with Adrian, Michael, the writers, and the executives about the storyline of *Starman*, creative agreement could not be reached. The project was shelved, the team laid off, all the energy evaporated. We said goodbyes, readjusted, and moved on.

That's Hollywood.

Chapter 25

"THIS SCRIPT IS WRITTEN ON TOILET PAPER"

Fortunately for me, Adrian kept me on to start reading and analyzing scripts in-between answering phones and doing clerical work for him. We read piles of scripts, unable to find a possibility, until one day a badly written screenplay called *Flashdance* surfaced, within which were some intriguing commercial kernels: *an eighteen year old girl working a man's job as a welder by day, dances at a local bar by night, and dreams that maybe one day she'll have enough courage to audition at the school of ballet.*

Someone exclaimed, "This script is written on toilet paper! Hire a new writer!" So we did.

Several writers worked on the script but none seemed to get it just right until Katherine Reback was brought on board as a new writer—and even though she ultimately didn't get any screenwriting credit (Joe Eszterhas did), she, in my opinion, is the one who put life and heart into the script.

Our many story/character meetings focused on themes: underdogs. Dancer's life. The big break. The project became a "go" at Paramount Pictures, then presided over by Dawn Steele.

"I need your cut within one year," she stated definitively.

"Bloody hell! That's impossible!" said Adrian, but he, as well as the producers, Jerry Bruckheimer and Don Simpson, agreed to her demand.

We moved into production offices at Paramount Studios. None of us had any idea about the future of this project.

I was constantly by Adrian's side, being his mediator, sounding board, errand runner, supporter, and red flagger, honored to learn daily about each department, each phase of the pre-production. I was disappointed when Adrian brought on another assistant to be his main assistant, but eventually understood the necessity, as the movie became more demanding on Adrian's time.

Chapter 26

FLASHDANCE

Day one of the casting call for the lead actress/dancer in *Flashdance* had been advertised in the trades. It was spring of 1984 and by 9 a.m., in blistering heat, hundreds of hopeful girls were already rushing onto the studio lot wanting to be at the front of the line.

Anticipation and excitement bubbled. The Hollywood dream. Maybe this audition would offer the break they had yearned for. What a sight! I was bowled over by the lines of beauties, all sizes, shapes, and ethnicities. I passed out water, enjoying the closer view of all the "costumes" which heightened sexuality and provoked attention. Frills and fringes, stripes and polka dots. Leggings of all colors, in primitive and psychedelic patterns, boasting shapely legs, muscular thighs and calves, five-inch stilettos and wedges, skintight leotards and tank tops flaunting cleavage and flat tummies.

Rhinestones, sequins, and beads gleamed in the sun. I gawked at one youngster, purple feathers interwoven through her long blond hair, wearing torn black fishnet stockings, scarlet high heels, and her voluptuous chest bursting out of a fluorescent green skimpy tank top. Silver-studded black leather cuffs on her wrists, masses of bangles and bracelets were bunched together on her arm. She waved flirtatiously to studio workers who slowed down in their electric buggies to ogle this spectacular display of femininity and sexuality.

When Sylvester Stallone came on the lot, surrounded by three or four bodyguards, and when he and his men passed by the lines, the girls squealed, yelled his name, jumped up and down. He waved back with a broad smile, blew kisses. More screaming. He made their day!

On the stage, girls were dismissed almost immediately. Not the "right look" or they were asked to read lines, sometimes one line only, sometimes two pages. Possibles were videotaped. We had boxes of Polaroids for reference. The casting call continued for days. Thousands of girls auditioned in L.A. and in other major U.S cities. But a seasoned actress with dancing talent, or a dancer who had the potential to act, could not be found.

Finally, the focus was on Jennifer Beals, pending screen tests, which went well. She was believable as a welder in a blue-collar environment, working in a man's world; sweet, authentic, and sexy as a dancer in a steelworker's hangout bar, Mawby's. Her tests got positive votes from Adrian, Jerry Bruckheimer, Don Simpson, Dawn Steele, and the host of studio executives, though everyone continued to express doubt about the film's future.

Jennifer expressed her motivation to work with the choreographer, Jeffery Hornaday, to gain more dance training. I liked Jennifer. She was unpretentious, easy-going, and smart. Whenever time allowed, she sat by herself reading the classics, her goal being to attend Yale to study literature. She performed the screen tests well, but we still had not found the male lead, the boss who becomes her lover. A temporary substitute actor would play the stand-in until the actual role was cast. An unknown, Kevin Costner, was given the job.

During read-throughs and rehearsals, whenever we had the time, Kevin and I, often joined by others, would escape the Craft Services (the food supplied by the production), at the time mostly junk food, and tromp off to Nickodell Restaurant on Melrose Avenue, just outside Paramount Studios, for Caesar salads.

Kevin was frustrated with being a stand-in. "My dreams soar beyond this," he'd complain.

"You're getting noticed," I'd remind him, trying to be encouraging.

"I guess I should be glad to be working at all."

"You have a classy Gary Cooper demeanor, and a low-key style and sexuality about you. And you can act! You'll become a big star! I predict it."

"That'll be the day, but thanks for your confidence!"

Of course, within a few years of this conversation, Kevin had become a world-famous actor, director, and producer, well-liked, gracious, and bankable. His film, *Dances with Wolves*, earned seven Academy Awards. How quickly things can change — for the better, or for the worse.

Marine Jahan, a talented dancer, close to Jennifer's height and build, was chosen to dance for Jennifer when necessary. It was a creative decision and an exciting combination which "worked." Jeffrey Hornaday worked on intense dance sequences with Marine, and movement with Jennifer. The music, by Giorgio Moroder, started to form, rousing, catchy, and slick, both for the club scenes and the ballet audition.

Our tight budget and one-year deadline were pressure. Adrian asked me to help out in overloaded departments, which allowed me to step into every phase of the production. I assisted Bobbie Read, the costumer and a fellow Brit, in search of outfits for Jennifer.

Bobbie had straight blond hair, bangs that almost covered her eyes, a thick East London cockney accent, and was modest with an impish, sometimes sarcastic, sense of humor. I told her that she could easily "make it" in the comedy club circuit.

I followed Bobbi around, trying to pick up her taste for Jennifer's "look," but she said, "Annie, think unique. What grabs you? Have some fun with it!"

"Like I know clothes!"

But I learned. I chose items as we scoured through racks and racks, holding them up for Bobbi's nod of approval. We kept buying armfuls of clothes for small change in resale stores, vintage shops, and donation centers all over the city.

I worked a tiring twelve to fifteen hours daily, but I was thrilled to be working on the film. I helped with the auditioning for the as-yet unfilled male lead; Michael Nouri was finally cast. The designer remodeled the interior of a bar in downtown LA, which would become our "Mawby's," the steelworker's beer hangout and a perfect setting for the raucous response to the sexy flash dancers.

With the casting of Nouri, it was a wrap for Kevin. His job was over.

"I know I'll see you on the screen soon," I said sincerely.

Kevin grinned and shrugged his shoulders. "At least I have one fan."

We hugged and said farewell.

Flashdance was completed after eighteen intense months and a nervous extension from Dawn Steele. When we finally got a rough cut, we rounded up two hundred young people from the Westwood Village area of LA near UCLA to see the first cut of the film at the studios. We were all nervous at the outcome, convinced the reviews would add up to a big flop. But no, it was magnanimous praise. We were bowled over.

After production, I escaped to Hawaii to recuperate. I was exhausted.

I was also excited as the film opened across the country and was such a success. When I ventured out of my hotel after sleeping for days, I heard the soundtrack of *Flashdance* blaring out from shops and restaurants, mainly *What a Feeling*. Torn tees or sweatshirts adorned mannequins in shop windows. None of us thought our film would be so successful, never mind become a smash hit! I was thrilled!

While still in Hawaii, I was suddenly treated like a celebrity, answering questions about *Flashdance* and then given the key to the spacious penthouse suite, a fancier room with a panoramic view of the beach and ocean for no extra charge. I was wrapped in contentment, a feeling I had yearned for most of my life. *How could one maintain such a pleasant state of mind?* I wondered.

I ventured further along Waikiki Beach to discover surfing, hikes to waterfalls, hip clubs, hula lessons, museums, and dining options from noodles to elegant menus.

By the time I returned to L.A I was rejuvenated.

And once again, I was out of work in Hollywood.

My father would surely have something to say about that.

Chapter 27

THE DEATH OF ORSON WELLES

D riving in Hollywood a few months later, a news bulletin interrupted a Mozart piano concerto on my car radio: "Orson Welles died of a heart attack at his home in Hollywood today, October 10th, 1985. He was an icon in filmmaking, and people all over the world were awed by his genius and larger-than-life personality."

His death left me stunned. I sat frozen in my driveway, still unable to comprehend the news. The announcer's voice repeated in my mind. "Orson Welles died of a heart attack." Stricken with numbness, I finally sobbed for the loss of this extraordinary man, whom I had been lucky to know and work with.

Later that night when I was calmer, I remembered that Orson had suggested twice that when we returned to L.A., I join him for lunch at his special table at the chic Hollywood restaurant, *Ma Maison*. I was awed by his invites. But for some unknown reason, I never arranged to meet him there. I regret not going, because I had always wanted to express how much I had learned from him, not only about filmmaking but about people, seeing them through his eyes, the way he interacted with them, and they with him. Because of his often domineering personality, I learned how to be assertive. I became strong and teasing, refusing to be intimidated, whomever the celebrity. I learned quickly after being hired by him that he respected those who treated him as a real person, not as a genius filmmaker.

At times after that, I was able to hear Orson, as though he were standing in the room with me. Direct, cutting, and furious, other times tinged with laughter or amusement, though brusque nonetheless. I will never forget his bellowing voice, his confidence, power, authority, even genius, all evident through the way he directed and communicated with actors and employees, growing louder if his meaning wasn't conveyed the first time.

Along with his voice, I can remember the smell of his cigar and how plumes of smoke would gather at the ceiling as we went over the day's activities. It never bothered me — in fact, I had liked his constant puff, puff, puffing at the cigar, unless Orson became distracted, in which case it burned steadily in a nearby ashtray. Discarded, but not forgotten.

Not having had that lunch with Orson is my only real regret in my life. He was one of my few mentors and I will always treasure my time spent with him. I had so much to tell him about all he had taught me — about filmmaking, about celebrities and how to deal with them, about how to say no to people, including celebrities — and ultimately how to believe in myself. He had such faith in me. And I never got to thank him. He really wanted to have that lunch. He called twice. But for one reason or another I couldn't arrange it. Then it was too late. It's a huge regret. A universal regret. One to learn from.

Chapter 28

MELTDOWN

It was Saturday morning, a beautiful day in sunny Los Angeles, California. I had been doing my weekly supermarket shopping, cruising past the cheeses, weighing fruits and vegetables, combing the aisles. I stopped to survey the selection of Campbell's soups, and searched for my favorite, green pea and ham. But suddenly, all the labels started swirling and blurring before my eyes. I blinked, then again, and tried shaking my head for clarity, yet I was unable to focus on anything. Everything spun faster and faster.

Intense fear swept through me. Shortness of breath, racy pulse, pains in my chest, and dizziness. Was I going crazy? Perhaps I was suffering a heart attack. Would I collapse and expire in front of the soups? I went with my first instinct: get out of the store!

After abandoning my shopping basket, I staggered outside. I reached for carts, arranged in two straight lines outside of the grocery mart door, for the wall, for whatever seemed stationary enough to steady me. My body was shaking. I felt terribly ill, and I was growing increasingly more terrified of fainting. I collapsed onto a bench, my head down between my legs, and took deep, slow breaths. My pulse slowly evened out with every exhalation, until about fifteen minutes later, when the symptoms began to fade.

Shattered and exhausted, I glanced around the parking lot, relieved that my dizziness had abated.

What had happened to me? Was I going mad?

"Sounds like you had a panic attack," said my pal later that day. "Let me give you the name of my psychotherapist. Maybe she can help you figure out why this happened."

"A shrink? You mean talk about myself to a complete stranger?" I asked, aghast.

"Yes. Do yourself a favor, Annie." She rummaged through her wallet for the information.

"It would be a waste of time and money. Don't worry, I'm okay now," I protested. But I took the business card she handed me.

"It could be something, it could be nothing. Don't you owe it to yourself to find out?" She left me with those few final words of wisdom.

Over the next several days I tried to convince myself that I was "back to normal." I knew I wasn't, and I worried that the incident would recur. I finally decided that I had nothing to lose by making an appointment with Angela, the psychotherapist. One chat would bail me out of my wimpy state.

Chapter 29

I WANT TO DO WHAT *YOU* DO

Three days later, even as I was driving to the therapy center, I was debating with myself about whether or not I should keep the appointment. I had been in such a dither, not like me at all. Why was I so reluctant, even fearful, of keeping the appointment? Or was I being practical, not wanting to waste my time or hers? In England, it had been drummed into my head that one had to be "mental" to see a shrink. But in Hollywood, seeing a therapist regularly seemed to be the thing to do for overall emotional health.

Wasn't it a violation of one's privacy, I wondered? Shrinks had power and authority. If the psychotherapist diagnosed me with a mental disease, she could lock me up in a loony bin. My head continued to run around in zigs and zags until I was in the parking lot of the California Family Study Center. Waves of anxiety bombarded me. Dizziness swiftly followed. Oh no. Not again! I breathed deeply and mustered the courage to leave the safety of my car.

Why are you doing this, Annie? A judgmental voice bellowed in my mind as I ventured inside.

A young bloke, muttering and distraught, brushed past me through the lobby doors. A cloud of anxiety hung around him that further strained my unsettled nerves. My apprehension was made worse by the incessant wailing of two young children, who were accompanied by their teenage mother. The family was being led to the desk by a calm looking chap, presumably their therapist, to set another session. It was not the place for me, I decided.

I was about to escape the insanity when my name was called. Drat, too late.

Angela introduced herself with a warm voice and a firm handshake. I followed her down the narrow, undecorated hallway to her office. She closed the door and I found myself in a dreary, spartan room. There was no window and only one picture on the wall. Why only one? Surely another landscape, seascape, anything, would cheer up the dungeon-like surroundings. I swallowed my nerves, forced a smile, and slumped down into one of the two sludge-green armchairs. I was not usually at a loss for words, but I wasn't sure how to proceed. Just like my mother, I felt an overwhelming need to break the silence.

"How can I help you, Annie?" Angela asked.

"I'm not sure," I replied hesitantly.

"Our intake states that you became dizzy and almost fainted in the supermarket?"

I nodded, not wanting to remember the incident. I couldn't recall ever being as self-conscious. Her gaze unnerved me, though she seemed kind and caring. I had always envisioned therapist types as being rather old-fashioned and dowdy, but she wore low, black suede heels, a simple feminine black suit, and a crisp white shirt. Classy.

"Any clues as to why that episode happened to you?" she asked.

"None."

Recognizing my reticence to talk, Angela shifted subjects to ask me about why I had left England. Finding that subject much easier to talk about, I blurted out some of my reasons for leaving my home country.

"I was nineteen and I felt stifled, impossibly restless. I felt that same restlessness and dissatisfaction at ten years old. It was time for a change. I was surrounded by complacency and wanted more, more opportunities, adventure. I feel free to be myself in LA, to follow my dreams and not be judged."

I explained that there were no rigid social roles to abide by in the States of the kind that had been ingrained in me during my British upbringing. In England, I had wondered if people spoke in secret codes. I was convinced that all of the impersonal chatter had deeper levels of meaning. People would say one thing but mean another. I was mystified. British reserve and banal chatter made communication in L.A. seem more open, more real and stimulating.

Angela admired my strength and courage in leaving my home and country. I shrugged. Her eyes never left my face. Mine wandered around the room, anything to avoid eye contact with her as she continued to scrutinize me.

"Have you made any changes in your daily routine?" she asked.

"Not really...," I thought for a bit. "Well, yes..."

I told her about Kit, even though it had been years since he died. As I was describing Kit's death, I experienced waves of nausea. Dizziness. *Oh no, not again...*

"What are you feeling?" Angela asked.

"I'm passing out..."

"I think you're starting to have a panic attack, probably just as you did in the market. Look at me. Breathe deeply and slowly. Breathe as though your lungs have dropped into your tummy."

Angela was blurry in my sight, but I tried to copy her as she placed her hand on her stomach, breathing deeply, her hand moving back and forth. We sat in silence for a few moments.

"Continue to deep breathe and your pulse will slow way down. You'll feel better."

She was right. My symptoms slowly abated. I was reassured by her confidence. Her expression became comforting to me. She explained the nature of panic attacks and of other ways to cope with them. The session ended after a fast fifty minutes.

Despite my discomfort, I admitted to myself that Angela's support and guidance had left me calmer, and with practical knowledge of ways to cope in the event of another attack.

For the next eighteen months, Angela became my weekly emotional detective, exploring with me my upbringing, my family relationships, my life in England, my desires to emigrate, my successes, my losses, and primarily my grief over the death of Christopher, something I had never dared address head-on. I had masked feelings about his death. Anger. Rage. Grief. Unconsciously searching for and wanting to recreate that relationship. A futile search. There could never be another Christopher. I started to truly grieve the loss of my true love. To this day, I avert my eyes from any drowning sequences on film, or when thrill-seekers take turns diving off boulders into the river or ocean.

Despite my ravaging pain, I knew that life needed to continue, and that I had to find work in order to maintain my lifestyle, having depleted that savings account I'd been so proud of. I could not let everything go to hell. Christopher and I had promised one another that, no matter what might happen, we would do our best to continue on with our lives.

I had avoided the search for self-awareness throughout my life, focusing outward by judging others, England, and how to escape my life. But now the content of each session with Angela lingered in my head over the next week, and once in a while a piece of the puzzle of how I became the way I was surfaced, and became something I reflected on carefully, eventually accepting or discarding the changing perspectives. Often the information was startling.

During one of our sessions, in the midst of exploring my ongoing problem of being overly judgmental, I was stunned by a sudden revelation:

"Angela," I blurted out, "I want to do what *you* do. And I want to specialize in working with people in the film business."

Chapter 30

CAL-FAM

I had shocked myself by this spontaneous insight, which dropped out of the blue sky. I become motivated to truly embrace this goal. I became even more frugal, saving money for my education but often wondering if I could sacrifice all the time, money, and dedication it would take to be a student again. I researched all of the master's programs in the area, attended orientations at various psychological institutions to acquire a sense of the teachers, the subjects, and the expectations. Months later, I decided that I would feel fulfilled guiding and supporting clients through their pain, just as Angela had done for me.

Surprisingly, especially for Hollywood, celebrity stress had not yet been studied. The *L.A Times* would later report that my thesis, titled, *The Occupational Stress of Working in the Film Business: The Effects on the Individual, His/Her Partner, and Family*, was the first of its kind, "...blazing new territory."

Early in 1987, I chose the California Family Study Center (now called Phillip's Graduate Institute) in Encino, California, for its emphasis on family counseling, geared toward self-growth and development. I completed the long application with shaking hands, and later learned that I had been accepted as a student for the two year master's training.

On the first day of class, I saw that the students were much younger than I. I plonked myself next to a girl about my age, Loni, with short, spiked hair, wearing a white sweatshirt like mine, hand painted and with glittery designs. We had similar visions of the world and became close pals. Like naughty teenagers in class, we drew cartoons of the teachers, passed notes to each other, giggling. We had discussions and disagreements about the lectures, learning about ourselves in the process. Our main anxiety stemmed from writing papers about a particular theorist and how his theories related to our lives.

Doing therapy with a client in front of the class for the first time was terrifying. We used a two-way mirror, then had the class critique the session.

I loved it, *all* of it.

The accelerated program enabled me to work part-time, which I arranged through Columbia Pictures, doing temporary jobs for producers and executives despite the drudgery of arranging meetings, answering phone calls, making coffee, but often the assignments gave me freedom to study.

After completion of my master's degree in marriage and family therapy in late 1989, I was accepted into two internship programs, one affiliated with the school, the other working in a group home for teenage boys on probation from jail. I had sought internships which would pay some money as well as offer experience with different kinds of clients.

When I started these positions, I began hearing about the Board of Behavioral Science Examiners (BBSE), located in Sacramento, the state capitol.

"Who is on this Board?" I asked the other interns at lunch one day.

"All we know," said Loni, "is that these eleven or twelve people *rule* over our profession."

"I've heard they can be ruthless if you ever cross them," said another.

I researched the BBSE and found that this governing group rules over all policies, procedures, and decisions about a therapist's actions. Its mission is "to protect and serve Californians by enforcing standards for safe and competent mental health practice." The Board's way is to "be a person of integrity, be professional and dedicated, and serve with excellence." I was proud to practice those principles, and thought, *I am. I do. And I will.*

About half of the Board is made up of people in the field of psychology, and the others are public members, appointed by the governor. The Board develops statutes and regulations, structures the oral and written examinations, verifies licenses, and investigates complaints against any *individual* therapist.

Over a two-year period, each intern had to complete three thousand hours of supervised clinical work with a designated number of weekly sessions with families, couples, adults, and children. We had to carefully track our meetings with these clients in sessions with our licensed supervisors, as well as in the group supervision meetings in which participants presented and discussed cases for feedback and guidance. Each session had to be detailed and signed off accurately.

The requirements were specific, but, at times, difficult to understand, necessitating telephone calls to the Board of Behavioral Science Examiners for clarification, which is what began my initial frustration with the BBSE. At that time, we interns were impatient with the Sacramento telephone number's constant busy signal, finally getting through only to be put on hold, and often cut off.

Chapter 31

A THERAPIST IS BORN

Initially during this intern period it was nerve-wracking being with clients on my own, but as I accumulated the hours, I became more at ease, and even slightly confident when I spoke with them.

One of my first clients as a supervised intern at the California Study Center was a twenty year-old, overweight, shy man who had relocated from Wisconsin to Los Angeles. Despite all the training to become a therapist, I sat there nervously wondering how to begin. I heard one of my teachers say, "Listen, and don't go ahead of the client." So I listened.

The client was confused about why he had come into therapy and immediately veered off into his love of ice hockey. He spent four full sessions educating me about the sport, giving me details about the players, teams, rules, positions. Everything. I sat there, interested, and asked questions when I could not understand his explanations. Internally, I was impatient to probe for issues. After every session, I fled to my supervisor for advice, yet again frustrated by our lack of progress.

"We are taking his money for therapy sessions, but all I am doing is listening to him talk about ice hockey. He won't touch upon anything. This is not therapy! Shouldn't we reassign him to a more experienced therapist?" I asked, hopefully.

"No, Annie! Hang in there with him. You are laying a foundation of trust. At some point, he will open up to you."

During our next two sessions, describing his experiences hunting elk, he let his guard down and began telling me about his friends, family and schools. I learned he had been very severely physically abused and tortured by his alcoholic father. The details of what he had endured made me weep inside, but provoked a newly found sense of compassion for him.

He stayed in therapy for almost a year, working through his grief, rage, sadness. I will never forget his strength and courage and how much I learned from him as a beginning therapist.

After two and a half years of practicing therapy, I had finally accrued the hours required in each category and learned about myself and my clients during the sessions. I was ready to submit my application package to the Board of Behavioral Science Examiners. If accepted, I would be eligible to start the examination process. I went over the math and scrutinized every form over and over again. Each one was signed by a supervisor and dated, but what if I had omitted a crucial detail? What if the estimations of my hours were inaccurate? If my application was rejected, my eligibility to take the written and oral examinations would be delayed for at least a month or more. I finally mailed in the stack of paperwork, return receipt requested.

Then I waited. I rushed to the mailbox each night. Nothing.

Finally, a letter from the Board arrived, accepting my application. I had successfully completed the first phase, and was now ready to move on to the grueling process of studying for the written test, which had a reputation of being extremely difficult with a low "pass" rate; a tricky four-hour test and a wait of several weeks to get the results.

At last, another letter arrived informing me that I had passed the written exam and would be eligible for the next scheduled oral exam to be held in several weeks.

On the appointed day, I sat in the waiting room along with a number of others. We were all terrified, venting our insecurities and anxiety to one another as we awaited our personal appointments with three examiners. We wondered who the examiners were, and how they were chosen.

Each of us went through an hour being grilled on our presented vignettes, then questioned about cases provided to us by them.

Back home, I waited for the results. A letter from the BBSE. I opened it up. In disbelief, I read and re-read the letter. I had passed! My license would arrive soon. I remained for hours in a happy state of shock.

The torturous process was over.

Part III
(2008-2011)

BACK TO...
The Unmaking of a
Hollywood
Therapist

Chapter 32

THE ATTORNEY

The drive home from the impound where I had picked up my car after my arrest and night in jail was harrowing. I kept checking the rearview mirror, terrified that a police car would appear behind me. I pulled into our driveway, drained. Though I yearned to crawl into bed, I forced myself to research DUI attorneys on the Internet. There were hundreds of them in the area. After several hours, I focused on a firm of three, located near the Van Nuys jail. They were situated directly across from the courthouse, and had decades of DUI experience. I assumed they would have relationships with the judges and legal staff at the court. Immediately responsive, their office receptionist set an appointment for me that afternoon.

Bruce drove me to the law office. He was insistent on being there for me both emotionally and professionally, his experience in law a great comfort. In the busy lobby, I tried to calm my nerves by watching how the office was run. One of their employees was fielding phone calls, her voice experienced, yet drowned out by their noisy fax machine. Light flashed from underneath its panel as another assistant scanned and faxed documents.

David Kestenbaum, an energetic man in his late 40's, wearing a crisp striped shirt and a pink spotted bow tie, introduced himself to us and led us into his office. After a few personal questions, he asked me to recount the details of my DUI arrest. Bruce nodded succinctly at me, giving his approval.

Kestenbaum listened intently, without having me feel as though he judged me for my mistake, and then outlined his expectations about what would unfold: my trial date, driving license suspension, and his estimation of the fees. His details were welcome, yet deep down, I only needed to know one thing. Would I be returned to jail?

"This is your first DUI, Annie, and believe me, there will be costs to pay. But there are no legal grounds for you to be incarcerated again for this case," he said emphatically.

We hired David and paid his $5,000 retainer, clarifying his instructions about all the paperwork that I, and he, would need to send to the Department of Motor Vehicles.

On December 11th, 2008, the Superior Court issued an order, "*People vs. Annie Coe Toor*," that would "allow" me to enroll in a nine-month drug and alcohol program, held by the Driving Safety School. Disgust washed through me. How gracious of the Court, I thought sarcastically.

I was to be prosecuted by the Los Angeles City Attorney Office, who had already informed the Department of Motor Vehicles of my crime. My temporary license was set to expire thirty days after my arrest, which had been on November 11th, 2008.

Chapter 33

TELLING JACQUIE

Though I had been assured I wouldn't be returning to jail, I was truly frightened about what would happen to me professionally. I didn't know what would become of my reputation, my successful business, and all of the clients who had trusted me and had invested their time with me.

I was not emotionally strong enough to tell my close friends about my situation. The pervasive shame remained with me. Needing someone I could implicitly trust, I called my sister. I paused, the phone receiver in hand, trying to decide how to tell her. It would be shocking to her, and I fretted between direct admittance, or perhaps a slower revelation.

"Jacquie here," she answered.

"Hello, Jacquie."

"Annie! Hi! How are you?"

"I've been in jail overnight for a DUI," I uttered quietly into the receiver.

Her compassion nearly brought me to tears. She listened and asked questions, hearing me with her heart, wrapping me in her love and acceptance.

"Please guard my secret, Jacquie. No one else must know what happened. I've lost all sense of myself and I cannot risk sharing this ugliness, even to my closest friends." Words poured out of me, barely coherent, but that's why I called my sister. I didn't need to make sense. I knew she would understand.

"You cannot move on until you forgive yourself, Annie. You have to stop being so cruel to yourself."

She was right. I had been ruthless, beating myself emotionally and spiritually. I needed to practice what I preached to my clients, and learn to regard my crime in a less self-critical way. It could have been a tragedy, a wreckage of vehicles, serious injuries of children and adults. I could have been charged with murder, or sentenced with a manslaughter charge, living the rest of my life behind bars. Yet I had not hurt anyone. By the end of our conversation, I felt my perspective changing. It was refreshing; I was no longer wallowing in as much doubt and despair.

Chapter 34

DRIVING SAFETY

My mailbox was swamped with lawyer pamphlets and stamped envelopes offering help with my DUI. I waited, nerve-stricken, for updates from David Kestenbaum. I was confused by the DMV's almost daily correspondences with me. "Your license has been revoked." A day or so later, "Your license has been reinstated."

I was ordered not to drive. How to exist in L.A. without driving? And yet the barrage of conflicting letters continued for over a month. Through persistent phone calls to my attorney and insurance agent, I found out the facts. I was aghast to learn that the insurance rates for both Bruce and me would be greatly increased. Our insurance company issued us an SR22 form, needing proof of my enrollment in an approved DUI/Driving Safety School.

The DMV demanded a re-issuance fee of $125.00 for my driver's license, and permitted me a restricted license, which enabled me to drive to DUI classes, AA meetings, and work.

When David received the actual Stipulated Settlement and Disciplinary Order from the Attorney General — thirteen pages detailing the Board's requirements — he immediately mailed it to me. The contents of the document were substantial and daunting. I had expected to feel relieved, but I was becoming increasingly disturbed.

The Board of Behavioral Sciences (the Board of Behavioral Science Examiners, BBSE, having morphed through various name changes, became the Board of Behavioral Sciences, BBS, in January of 1997) demanded that I abstain from the use of alcohol and submit to random biological fluid testing. I was liable to be pulled over and searched randomly, at any time. They would have me appear, in person, for an interview with them, or with their designee at various intervals. I was to send them quarterly reports, updating them on my compliance with my probation conditions. They would have me notify my clients when any term or condition of my probation would affect their therapy, or the confidentiality of their records.

I was able to continue seeing my clients (I didn't tell them what had happened to me) and to maintain a valid license throughout the probation period. The Board insisted I graduate from alcohol and drug education to meet their required two semester units. They would also enforce regular psychotherapy sessions with a therapist, approved by them. Their letter ended with a bill of $2,600 for the cost of their investigation and prosecution of my case. If any of the probation conditions were violated, the Board, after giving me the opportunity to be heard, could revoke my license to practice my profession.

Three whole years under those conditions? And *one* violation could mean stripping me of my therapist's license? I was disgusted to the core. My professional and personal record had been impeccable all my life. I found the terms to be abusive and demeaning. To be treated like a hardened criminal, and to be under Big Brother's jurisdiction for three years, felt intolerable — as though I were a juvenile delinquent. No one had ever tried to limit my freedom or control my life in such a way.

My nine-month DUI program required attendance in thirty-eight group sessions, nineteen biweekly individual sessions, twelve hours of film education classes and twenty Alcoholics Anonymous meetings where the goal was to encourage people to overcome their addiction to liquor by placing one's faith and trust in a "higher power." It was to be done by attending regular meetings, finding a sponsor, working the Twelve Steps and becoming dedicated to being sober, which I eventually did.

At the first driving safety class, I glanced around at the sixteen other offenders, all of whom behaved as though they hadn't committed a crime. They were, for the most part, scruffy individuals, some sporting gang attire, all of them glued to their cell phones, texting, talking, boastfully telling their stories involving alcohol. I fell into a heavy state of depression, no longer feeling any motivation to stay. Fortunately, a slim girl about my age, with eye-catching, long red hair, beckoned for me to sit next to her. Fiona, fiercely honest and feisty, quickly became my friend. We had both spent years in show business, she as a top agent for actors, me working for directors in development, or on films, and then as a psychotherapist specializing in clients in film. We had lots to gab about, a good distraction from the potential sociopaths in our group.

She and I wanted to learn from the sessions, but each meeting was the same. The leader asked: *How did your DUI happen? How many offenses have you committed? Are you an alcoholic? Are you still drinking, now? Tell us about the history of your alcohol usage.* Not surprisingly, their mechanical questions received lackluster responses. As AA attendees, Fiona and I tried to vitalize and improve the sessions, though we were careful not to usurp the leaders and risk even more blemishes in our records.

A new member joined the group, dressed in a different three-piece suit each session. He was a medical doctor who had a haughty way of describing his history with alcohol. He had been convicted of ten DUI offenses.

Fiona and I stared at each other in disbelief, more so when he told the group that his daily ritual was to stop into the bar a block from his office for a shot of vodka before seeing his morning patients. A doctor! The Hippocratic Oath apparently meant nothing to him. We were outraged to learn that, despite his long history of offenses, he had only spent seventy-five days in jail. Two of his friends, judges, "pulled strings" for him, he boasted.

After the end of every DUI class, Fiona and I escaped outside to breathe deep sighs of relief. We made a contract with one another: we would never, ever, drink and drive again.

"We must help each other to forgive ourselves," I said.

"We have to, and we will," replied Fiona.

I was developing a sense of contentment that I was fulfilling the state's requirements, not drinking, and feeling slightly better about myself. But a pervasive restlessness about my future haunted me.

Chapter 35

TEMPORARY REPRIEVE

On July 21st, 2009, my psychotherapy license renewal form arrived in the mail, as it did every two years. A short questionnaire was always included. My heart thumped with dread at the question, "Have you been convicted of a crime since your last renewal?"

I wanted to lie. I spent the next several days soul-searching, weighing the consequences a lie might cause. Surely, one DUI on my otherwise impeccable record would not warrant a harsh response. I had paid my dues, attended the classes, and continued to work through the Los Angeles court debacle. Surely the Board had no jurisdiction over me when I hadn't hurt any clients. My practice had not been involved in any way. There was no reason for the Board to step in. Or was there? I finally checked the "Yes" box, which required a three line explanation. I agonized as I wrote and rewrote a succinct description of my DUI. With trembling hands, I placed the envelope into the mailbox. I was proud of myself for not fabricating.

After several weeks, my license arrived in the mail. It had been renewed! I framed it in its place on my office wall to celebrate an end to my personal ugliness. I was able to breathe again. My stomach relaxed and I was more rested when I woke. Even my cats seemed to sense my renewed energy. They bounded around the house again, trailing at my feet wherever I went. Though I had two more months of driving safety classes to attend, I was able to see many clients daily. I relearned confidence, and even experienced glimmers of happiness again.

Throughout this whole period, Bruce was always interested in any new information I received about the case. He was interested in a kind of academic way, not in the frantic way that I had become invested in it. He was always supportive, always willing to give me his opinion. He was always there. My rock.

Chapter 36

THE BOARD FROM HELL

On October, 2009, I notified the Van Nuys Court of my completion of the DUI Safety Education Training, all the groups, individual sessions, and classes. I had logged over a hundred AA meetings and found a sponsor for support. I eventually admitted that I was powerless over alcohol, and that my life had become unmanageable. I was sober and not missing alcohol. Once all of the classes and group sessions were over, my schedule became much lighter. I felt more independent.

Five weeks later, while sorting through the mail, bills, workshop fliers, and advertisements, I saw an envelope from the BBS (formerly the BBSE). Instantaneously, my positive mood spiraled into a dark abyss. My name and address were personally printed, so this wasn't part of a mass mailing. Terrified of facing its content, I finally gathered courage and tore the letter open and read it with shaking hands and beating heart:

The Board was requesting a certified copy of my conviction, including police reports, proof of the fees and fines that I had paid to the Court, and a detailed description of my DUI. They also asked for a description of my rehabilitation efforts to prevent future problems. I was to send the information to the Law Enforcement Division headquarters.

If I failed to comply, the Board threatened to proceed with disciplinary action. I had written my statement on my renewal form. I wondered if they had lost it.

Seeing my distraught emotional state, Bruce sat down with me to read the letter for himself.

"I wish I had lied," I confessed.

"I understand how you feel. Maybe more details will appease them, then you can finally put the incident to rest."

"Maybe," I said, resting my head on his shoulder.

"Let's hope for the best," he answered with reassurance.

When I filled out the form the Board was now requesting, I wrote an accompanying note that I had received a DUI after a drink with an old friend, someone I had met while working on Katrina. I stressed that no clients were affected, and that no one else was involved and no car accident had occurred.

The Board, which purported to "provide excellent customer service to all its constituents" had, I felt, acted against their own credo in their treatment of me. I had spent hours on the phone trying to talk with a real person, and the few times that I did, I was treated brusquely, information about my case was withheld, or I was simply cut off the telephone line.

My therapist friends were all shocked to learn about my experience and the charges against me. My attorney, Michael, reassured me that I had an impeccable career, and after scrutiny of my life in private practice, he concluded "Annie, I think you are being set as an example — or scapegoated."

After reading through countless drafts of my detailed DUI description, I mailed it, along with the documentation they needed.

Several weeks passed. Nothing. Feeling helpless and insulted, I decided to take action. *Control your temper*, I warned myself before calling the Law Enforcement Division at the headquarters in Sacramento to find out the status of my case.

"Your letter is in a stack of others," the woman said harshly.

"But weeks have gone by. How much longer before I receive a response?"

"I have no idea."

"Is there anything I can do to expedite the process?" I asked desperately.

"Nothing. Wait." Cold, uncaring.

I was outraged, feeling positively abused by the Board. I was disgusted by their lack of responsibility. My worry caused physical symptoms. I was constantly tired after being wide awake most every night. Dark circles appeared under my eyes, which concealer could no longer disguise. My colleagues expressed concern about my weight loss, but my appetite remained poor, food having lost all of its taste. I forced myself to take daily walks, an activity that passed the time, not the crisp refreshing strolls I had taken in the past. Whenever I looked into a mirror, I was unable to believe the sight staring back at me: pale, gaunt, frazzled. My world had dwindled down to obsessing about each day's mail delivery. I was able to focus on sessions with my clients, yet couldn't muster the energy to see friends or family. Realizing I needed help with my depression and anxiety, I visited my doctor and described my symptoms. She immediately recommended an antidepressant, which I gladly accepted.

Periodically, I checked in again with the Law Enforcement Division for information, but the lack of response from the Board continued. I was always told, "Just wait," and had been rudely cut off at times.

I started to lose track of time. I couldn't remember when I ate, and couldn't be sure I had. My doctor recommended an increase to the dosage of my antidepressants. The cats gave me withering looks and stayed close to me, extra affectionate, yet more still and quiet than they usually were. Instinctive animals, sensitive to discord and pain, I would always be grateful to them for their understanding. Their quiet companionship was one of my main consolations.

Chapter 37

THE SLAM

My life continued to be "on hold" for yet another six months. I finally received an 8 x 10 envelope from the Department of Justice for the State of California. It was cold from being outside in the metal mailbox, and I myself felt chilled to the bone when I saw the sender. Its contents bore information that could change my life.

I was horrified to read: *"Accusation and Disciplinary Order before the Board of Behavioral Sciences, Department of Consumer Affairs, State of California, in the Accusation against Annie Coe Toor..."*

Bottom line: They intended to revoke my license to practice psychotherapy.

I made countless calls to the headquarters, which offered me only frustration and anger. I was nauseous, shaking in horror and rage. How could they have made the decision so callously, after I had met all their requirements? Now they wanted more? It wasn't fair!

A wave of heat suffused my body. Primal anger made me want to demand a private audience with the BBSE. After decades of seeking, I had finally found peace and fulfillment in my beloved career as a psychotherapist. It had been worth the thousands of dollars and all the time needed to obtain the necessary education. I had worked hard to achieve success, even some celebrity, in my practice.

As therapists, we are trained in empathy. We are taught to accept people for their faults, while trying to help them. Yet the most powerful people within the profession could not offer the same to those under their jurisdiction. I had finished the Superior Court's requirements, but was enraged that I now had to fight for justice.

When I felt calmer, I contacted my attorney, David Kestenbaum, for guidance. He referred me to a colleague, Michael Goch, who specialized in working with professionals in healthcare whose licenses were in jeopardy.

Bruce and I make an urgent appointment to see him that afternoon.

Michael's office was situated in a tall, glass building in Woodland Hills. Driving alongside the reflective shiny glass windows, in my mind I could see lawyers smartly dressed in three-piece suits, ties, briefcases in hand. Appearances weren't everything, but they certainly helped.

I admired the architecture of the building as we walked through its doors into the elevator. In Michael's waiting room, I again appreciated Bruce's calm presence whilst my heart jumped, hands and feet fidgety. I distracted myself with the antique wooden-framed comical etchings on the walls. Simple, yet with a touch of personality that surprised me in a place I hadn't expected to find humor.

Ten minutes passed. I listened to the lights hum, paced, tapped my foot in impatience. When I heard the door open, I turned to see a 6' 5 man stride into the room. An aura of sophistication, confidence, and warmth emanated from this elegant figure as he stood before us.

Michael had straight white hair almost to his shoulders. I wondered whether he had come from a wedding, a funeral, or if this was normal work attire for him. It was a very classy ensemble, regardless. Dressed in a black suit, long black jacket, and a white stripy tie, he was a dramatic looking vision, welcoming us with a broad smile and a strong, masculine handshake.

After hearing my story and history, Goch reassured me that the Court would not revoke my license to practice psychotherapy, "Not with just one DUI and an impeccable professional record." His optimism, jovial demeanor, humor and years of experience impressed and heartened us.

Michael later contacted me with instructions to compile a "discovery package" to respond to a Request for Discovery issued by the Attorney General's Office and to be utilized by us to show my qualifications and good standing.

The package contained my publications, interviews, panels I was invited to speak on as an expert working with celebrities, my Katrina honorary certifications from the Red Cross, radio, TV and newspaper interviews, diplomas of my numerous crisis trainings, and perhaps most weighty of all, eleven admiring declarations of my professionalism and ethical behavior from colleagues who were psychiatrists, therapists, and social workers, all of whom had many years of experience. Michael declared the package to be "quite impressive."

The Board decided to settle.

A win, I thought.

The Deputy Attorney General outlined the following settlement terms in a letter, which Michael had warned me to expect. Their bullet points, which read as follows, basically *doubled up* on everything I had already completed:

- Revocation stayed;
- 3 years' probation with standard terms and conditions;

- Education — alcohol and substance abuse, two semester units, graduate level;
- Personal psychotherapy;
- Abstain from use of alcohol;
- Reimbursement of probation program: $1,200 per year;
- Random biological fluid testing.

My immediate response was one of relief. I would keep my license! I called Michael.

Then I began having second thoughts. I called Michael again and asked that he argue with the Deputy Attorney General for less harsh conditions. He agreed, in spite of his pessimism.

Several days later, Michael informed me that the City Attorney and the Board were unwilling to make any lenient changes. Thus, I did not have any other option but to accept the conditions.

"I don't want to settle. Let them take my license," I said, after receiving the news.

After a long pause, Michael asked, "Why, Annie?"

"There are even *more* conditions than there were before. Three more years of probation? The random testing?" I shuddered, imagining three more years under scrutiny.

"This is the career you've built for decades."

"I've been a therapist for over fifteen years. It's not as if I were just starting out. I'm almost sixty-five years old, and I want to be done with the Board."

"This is a very grave decision, Annie, and one I would hate for you to regret. The consequences for your future will be permanent. You're thinking of throwing your career away."

Never having encountered a client who worked with him to fight the system and then gave up, Michael expressed a caring concern for my future. He knew I was soon to vacation with my sister in Puerto Vallarta, Mexico. His advice for me was to lie on a beach, soak up the heat, and think profoundly about my decision.

I agreed I would.

And I did.

Chapter 38

DECISION IN PARADISE

Puerto Vallarta was paradise. I had visited many times over the years, yet despite the expansion of luxury hotels and shopping centers, it retained charm and beauty. The downtown area was reminiscent of an authentic Mexican village. Jacquie and I spent the first two days lazing about on the hotel's beautiful white sand beach. During the evenings, we strolled about the busy *malecon*, the main seafront street, delighting in the whimsical bronze sculptures, the cool ocean breeze, the gentle waves, and such brilliant sunsets. We walked through colorful, crowded shops, and lively restaurants where we enjoyed scrumptious Mexican meals.

On the third day, Jacquie and I went to the beach. I brought the wretched settlement document with me in my beach bag. We propped up in two lounge chair under a *palapa*, and I read through the terms again, yellow-lining the most offensive points. What a dark, repugnant way to live. I was outraged by the details. My Mexican breakfast rolled around within my stomach. I would have to accept their terms or surrender my license. Both choices seemed despicable. I covered my eyes with the papers and leaned back in my chair, and thought about the trajectory that got me here.

"Why don't I read it now?" asked Jacquie, who had been reading a book, but saw my state of anguish.

"Yes, yes, please. I'll walk in the sea to cool off and think."

I was struck with one overwhelmingly insistent desire: *get away*. I stumbled on the sand, but picked up speed. Soon I was at an all-out run, shifting sand becoming firmer as I reached the water line. I needed the rejuvenating salty sea air, and to know that Los Angeles was miles away. It was not until I turned around that I realized how far I had run.

Where was I?

I had walked the beach many times, yet I had never seen what lay before my eyes. The sand spit extended as far as I could see. There were birds of all kinds flocked together; egrets and cranes, pelicans, seagulls dipped and swooped in the air above. I felt excruciatingly sad, yet rapturously happy. An intense sensation of inner peace swept over me. I sat in the wet sand, watching the beauteous sight. Clarity was sparkling and bright. I felt free, hopeful, full of potential.

If I surrendered my license, I would never be able to see clients again. Well, so be it. I distanced myself from the pain of leaving my practice. I would continue volunteering my time for disaster relief work with the Red Cross, and I would have more time with Bruce. I would also have time to write. I could travel and pursue passions I had delayed for my career. I had wanted to take riding lessons, swim, exercise more, and have an active social life without being shackled to my phone and beeper. Surrendering my license would give me the time to do other kinds of volunteer work, too, which always felt fulfilling — help neglected animals, or volunteer at a children's hospital. For once, I would know what it was to have "leisure time," a luxury. It *would* be strange to be without a practice, not seeing clients, yet I felt newly determined to build a creative new life. The possibilities seemed endless.

But would I be fulfilled? Would my new lifestyle bring all I hoped it would? I would have to put to rest the reality of being stripped of my license, years of education and hard work washed away.

The alternative was to continue with clients, and to strictly adhere to the conditions of my probation. I could never forget even one bullet point, as outlined by the Deputy Attorney General's Disciplinary Order. One slip, such as forgetting to check in with my assigned probation officer before I left town, or forgetting to submit a quarterly report, would be a violation. While the Board would give me an opportunity to be heard, I did not hope they would listen to anything I had to say. They would revoke my license, or begin the tedious legal back-and-forth, which I honestly had not yet recovered from. Would I live in fear, unable to relax and live without bitterness? The black cloud would continue to loom over my soul.

"It is disgusting," Jacquie said the moment I returned. "*One* DUI leading to these punitive terms? They want you to follow all these terms for three more years? They're mad!"

"I think so, too," I answered, relieved by her response.

"I'm furious for you! I thought you served the Court's punishment. The nine-month driving safety program, all those classes. Now the robots on the Board want to strip you? They want to revoke your license? Is there anything that you have done without you telling me?"

"Nothing, nothing at all. The DUI. That's it. That's what led to this."

"But you've been a successful therapist for so many years, with a stellar reputation. How dare they demand three more years of probation? I'm really angry for you, Sis. No wonder you are distraught. Ever since I can remember, you've been independent, creating your life according to your beliefs and dreams. It's difficult for me to think of you living under all these rules."

"For me, too," I said, feeling appreciative of her understanding and support.

"I wish you weren't in this horrible dilemma."

"I won't be for long." Her concern and anger for me bolstered my spirits.

I smiled at the muscular, tanned beach waiter who had joined us, dinner menus in hand. I was hungry, a new urge after months of my stomach being in knots. Jacquie and I ordered the appetizer sampler, a tray of chicken, potato taquitos with a chipotle sauce and guacamole and chips, a margarita for Jacquie, mineral water with lime for me. Nothing could be more decadent than to have our evening meal served to us on a glorious beach.

With the sun past the horizon line, all seemed still for endless, stretching moments. I had twenty-four hours to decide what my fate would be. But the decision no longer seemed as daunting.

Chapter 39

C'EST FINI

Back in reality on the airplane home, I felt replenished after our week in Mexico, returning to Los Angeles with energy and optimism. I was happy to reunite with Bruce and the cats, the latter remaining aloof until I unpacked and settled back into my daily routine. I spent time with Bruce, showing him pictures from our trip, as well as memories. And I told him about the conclusion I had reached.

"I'm almost sure of my decision," I said, letting him know what I had decided.

"Annie, love, I will accept and respect whatever you decide. Only you can settle on the right thing to do for you. It's your life, your future."

Bruce had been by my side, with love and acceptance, since I had been arrested. He had never judged me, nor been harsh. I was awed by his constant support, guidance and patience, even when I was at my worst, depressed, irascible.

I called Michael's secretary and made an appointment to visit the office.

Anxiety swept through me as I drove west on the Ventura Freeway, Michael's warning repeating in my mind. *Was I making the right choice?*

I exited the freeway at Canoga Avenue. Within moments, I heard a police siren. Hastily checking my rearview mirror, I was horrified to see a patrol car's flashing red and blue light appear behind my car. I choked in fear; I trembled, perspiring, gasping. What had I done wrong? I pulled over, my hands on the steering wheel. The nightmare of my prior traffic stop, the alcohol tests, arrest, and hours in jail, were visibly recalled. Thankfully, the police car passed by me, other cars pulling to the side as he drove onward. After a swig of water, I started to giggle deliriously. I was free, not the victim to be chastised!

I parked in the lot of Michael's office, and made my way into the building, then the elevator. As I was shown to his office, I once again felt sure of my decision.

"Annie! It's great to see you again! Did you enjoy Mexico?" His broad smile was infectious, as was his sincerity. He wore black jeans, which accentuated his long legs, and a crisp white suit shirt.

"We had a marvelous time, thank you. I love Puerto Vallarta. I feel more relaxed than I have since the DUI."

Michael pushed a button on his phone, asking the secretary to bring in documents for me to sign. A prune-faced, elderly woman walked in to hand him the papers.

"Thank you," he said.

He kept them in front of him on his desk.

"Before I show you what you need to sign, I should ask you, what conclusion did you reach?"

I got right to the point.

"I've thought deeply about how I want my future to look. It's clear to me that I want to live my life on my terms and not anyone else's. I will not be dictated to and have my rights usurped."

Michael stared at me, a solemn expression on his face. "This is a grave decision. You will never be able to practice therapy again. The end of your career. That's what you want?"

"Yes, Michael. I've made up my mind. I don't want to be on probation. I want to surrender my license, and I feel at peace with my choice. In fact, I'm excited about the possibilities of a new future. I know your job is to save peoples' licenses, and you have given me your professional guidance and caring concern from the very beginning. I admire and respect you very much."

"I pray that you will never regret this major decision," he said, still shaking his head in disbelief. "I have never worked with a client who has obtained a settlement, and then decided against it."

"I understand your dismay. But I am absolutely sure, and at peace."

"Okay, then," he said, realizing that I would not budge on my choice. "I'll handle things from here, inform the Attorney General's Office, and contact you soon."

"Thank you. For everything. You are brilliant, caring and kind, and I will never forget all that you've done for me."

The new document was received by the Board. After waiting for five weeks, my paperwork was approved. As instructed, I surrendered my wall license and its renewal by certified mail on November 18, 2010, two years and six days after my DUI arrest. The signed receipt I received from them arrived on November 26th.

The March/April 2011 issue of *The Therapist* magazine that goes to all of the nearly 30,000 licensed marriage and family therapists in the state of California published the details of my arrest for public knowledge in their *Disciplinary Action* section. My professional record had been publicly tarnished, yet I learned to separate the unprofessional ugliness from my personal sense of triumph, and the pride I felt in my past career. *C'est fini.*

Chapter 40

THE "SPIDER" PAGE

At the end of February, 2011, the issue of *The Therapist* that I'd been dreading came out and went to every one of the nearly 30,000 licensed marriage and family therapists in the state of California — in other words, just about everybody I knew in my professional world. Some of my colleagues refer to this horrific section of the magazine, called *Disciplinary Actions,* as the "spider" page. I'm not sure where the term originated, but perhaps it's because once you're caught up in it, it's hard to get free.

Published in **THE THERAPIST***, Vol 23, Issue 2*
March/April 2011

DISCPLINARY ACTIONS:

Annie Patricia Coe, Marriage and Family Therapist. Disposition: By stipulated surrender of license and order, license surrendered and accepted by the Board. Effective December 2, 2010. Charge: Respondent admits the truth of each and every charge and allegation in the Accusation, agrees that cause exists for discipline and hereby surrenders her license for the Board's acceptance. Respondent has subjected her license to disciplinary action on the grounds of' unprofessional conduct in that the Respondent was convicted of a crime, which is substantially related to the qualifications, functions, or duties of a Marriage and Family Therapist as follows: On or about December 8, 2008, in a criminal proceeding, Respondent was convicted on her plea of nolo contendere to driving under the influence of alcohol. Respondent sentenced to three years of summary probation, fined, and required to attend a nine month licensed first offender alcohol and other drug education counseling program. The circumstances are as follows: On or about November 19, 2008, a California highway patrol officer observed Respondent driving a vehicle erratically on the freeway. Respondent was instructed to exit the freeway. Upon making contact with Respondent, the officer detected a strong odor of alcohol emitting from Respondent's vehicle, and Respondent's eyes were red and watery, and her speech was slurred. Respondent admitted to the officer that she had been drinking alcohol. There was also an open container of wine in her vehicle. Respondent was given field sobriety tests which she failed. Respondent was then transported to the police station for a breath test for driving under the influence of alcohol. The test revealed that Respondent had a BAC of 0.24 percent, three times the legal limit. Respondent has subjected her license to disciplinary action, on the grounds of unprofessional conduct in that the Respondent consumed alcoholic beverages, to the extent, or in a manner, as to be dangerous to herself and to the public in that she was driving under the influence of alcohol with a 0.24 percent BAC.

After reading this, I was sick for days and days. Making it even worse were the factual errors, such as the statement that *"There was also an open container of wine in her vehicle"* — when, in fact, the corked bottle was in the *trunk*, not in the vehicle itself. Legally, that makes a difference. It left me with the impression that the work of the BBSE had been sloppy.

Bruce would see me eyeing the magazine on the coffee table in the living room, and come over and hug me close.

"I guess I'm no longer your Jaguar of therapists," I said, feeling dreadful about how I must be such a disappointment to him.

"Unlicensed, perhaps, but still a Jaguar," he said.

Chapter 41

AFTERMATH

My dream of coming to America far exceeded my expectations. In America, I found courage, then finally, happiness. From working with the legendary Orson Welles, to the countless celebrities I encountered and worked with, many of them quite remarkable people, and then, of course, there was Bruce.

I had learned to overcome debilitating grief, and had seen the true range of what humanity has to offer. I had always been a restless soul, never thinking I would find peace. There were only two things I had wanted to accomplish: I wanted adventure, and I wanted to escape the monotony of a complacent '"normal" life.

In California, I reveled in adventures, my life never being unexciting or predictable. I had the opportunity to gain higher education ("A superior education is worth any sacrifice," as my father used to say), and after many years, eventually became a therapist. And a successful one.

Memories are imprinted in my mind, sounds I will never forget. When I walk through my garage and catch a myriad of scents as I unload groceries, I am thrust back to my childhood. I hear the sound of tools clinking against one another, with Dad leaning over the hood or propped up underneath the car with parts strewn across the concrete floor. He always refused to take the car to a mechanic, choosing to fix his old vehicles himself. I remember entire days which flew by as Mum brought Dad endless cups of tea, while I sat and handed him tools, trying to regulate his moodiness, sharing in his ultimate triumph. At the end of the day, Dad's hands would be nearly black from all of the grease. He would playfully threaten to smear his greasy hands on my face and clothes, but he never did.

The change in weather from autumn to winter, slight though it is in California, makes me think back to dreary, cold days in England, huddling under blankets for warmth, my feet freezing, trying to keep as warm as possible before heading out into another miserable downpour. Yet, on clearer days, I remember being struck breathless by the shades of England's emerald greens, the fields stretching for miles with breaks dotted along the land with church spires, woods, and country villages. Sometimes the blue sky seemed more of an ocean, reflecting every shade and tint of green spread out before my eyes. The sight could almost make the rainy days all worth bearing.

I think, too, of other scenes from long ago that still make me smile, especially the day of my parents' silver anniversary luncheon at a "posh" hotel in Chester, England, on the River Dee close to the Welsh border.

Aside from my parents and Jacquie, then eighteen, about twenty relatives and friends were there. My mother and father were by far the most elegant and handsome in the group, amidst all the fancy suits and ties and chic dresses. The tablecloth was crisp and white, embroidered with matching serviettes and four white flower arrangements evenly spaced down the center. Each place setting boasted an array of etched, silver cutlery, lined up perfectly like silver soldiers next to several sizes of crystal glasses. I had never attended such a formal affair—which utensil, which glass to use? I quickly decided to imitate my Aunt Alicia's impeccable table manners, which I knew would bail me out of making any unforgivable faux pas.

My Aunt Doris sat regally at the opposite end of the table from me, judgmental and austere — one of those British people I had a history of trying to provoke into a genuine reaction.

On this particular occasion I had announced loudly and purposefully to the waiter, *"A Bloody Mary, please!"*

Aunt Doris turned ashen, covering her forehead with her hand as if a swoon were imminent. Jacquie broke into giggles. My parents glared at me. Mum gathered herself quickly, and started to chat to a neighbor in her diplomatic and gracious need to smooth over any tension.

After a pause, my father leaned over to me and whispered, almost prophetically, "Annie! You are a cheeky girl, always trying to get a rise out of us. *No more alcohol for you."*

My home now is the Hollywood Hills. The views from across the mountains to the sea continue to inspire me, as swimming pools help rejuvenate me. Here is where I wrote this book.

For months while I was writing the book, my close friend, Julie, kept pestering me to read it, so when the proof copies finally arrived, I gave one to her

She called me the very next day. "Annie!" she exclaimed. "You should *never* have checked that renewal box! Why did you?"

For a moment I didn't even know what she was talking about. Then I remembered. Ah, yes, she was referring to the application from the BBSE (the name still makes me gag) for the regular bi-annual renewal of my psychotherapist's license. The application had included that fork-in-the-road question: *"Have you been convicted of a crime since your last renewal?"* I was to put a check in one of two little boxes. *Yes?* or *No?*

How I'd agonized over those boxes. How very badly I had wanted to lie. For days I'd delved into all the possible consequences of each choice, over and over again—*Yes?* or *No?*

At one point I'd thought of my father and his endless supply of phrases to live by, "Do the right thing, Annie, and let the chips fall where they may."

The chips have fallen. Julie was right. Had I checked "No," I might have avoided all this and still been in my elegant office, a "therapist to the stars." But I had checked "Yes," and then all hell had broken loose. Years of it. I was punished mightily for my choice, but it was "the right thing to do," leaving me with no guilt; my conscience is clear and I am comfortable in my own skin. I have no regrets.

At points in our lives, aren't we all faced with "little boxes" to check? — the moral dilemmas of daily life — *Yes?* or *No?*

I am, in fact, grateful for that pivotal moment in my life. Today, when I walk across the sun-warmed edge of a swimming pool, the sun's bright rays sparkling on the clear, crystal turquoise water, and I am magically drawn, perhaps as Christopher was, to dive into the pool, my skin already hot from being outside, and experience that chilly-at-first, then wonderfully comfortable sensation of being cocooned in silence.

As I disappear under the water's surface, I am at peace, happy, confident, and free.

END

About the Author

ANNIE COE TOOR

Born in England, Annie Coe, from the age of ten, dreamed of living in California. She finally immigrated to Los Angeles in 1965, working in pharmaceuticals and then in the movie industry where her first job was as the assistant to the genius director, Orson Welles. From there, Annie went on to other movie industry positions in story analysis, development, and for eighteen months she worked on the production of the hit film, *Flashdance*.

After a tragic loss, she sought grief counseling, which led her into what would become her new passion, a career as a licensed psychotherapist. After spending years obtaining the necessary degrees, credentials, and internship hours, and writing her master's thesis on the psychological stresses of working in films, she finally opened her private practice in Hollywood, specializing in the entertainment industry. She became well-known as an expert in that field, and gave many radio and television interviews on industry "stress." In addition, Annie spent a great deal of her time doing volunteer work, including crisis counseling for the Red Cross when hurricane Katrina hit New Orleans. She married Bruce Toor, an attorney, in 2000. At the zenith of her success as a therapist and a sterling reputation as a humanitarian, a single incident occurred one night that threw Annie totally off-track — and that is where *The Unmaking of a Hollywood Therapist* begins.

Author's Request

If you enjoyed **The Unmaking of a Hollywood Therapist**, or found it informative—or even a good warning — I'd be so grateful if you'd post a review on Amazon.com. Your support really does make a difference in spreading the word and getting the book to others who might also enjoy it or benefit from it.

To write a comment or review, go on the Amazon.com site, click on *Books* in the drop-down menu, and type in the name if this book. Once on my book page, click on the "Customer Review" option and a box should open up for you to write in your comment. Thank you!

— Annie Coe Toor

Contact Information:

www.TimberlakePress.com
info@TimberlakePress.com
Box 129
Woodland Hills, CA, 91365, USA

17801104R00125

Printed in Great Britain
by Amazon